INFINITE THOUGHT

INFINITE THOUGHT
Truth and the Return to Philosophy

Alain Badiou

Translated and edited by
Oliver Feltham and Justin Clemens

continuum

Continuum

The Tower Building
11 York Road
London, SE1 7NX

15 East 26th Street
New York
NY 10010

www.continuumbooks.com

Reprinted 2003
This paperback edition published 2005 by Continuum

British Library Cataloguing-in-Publication Data
A catalogue record for this book is available from the British Library

ISBN 0–8264–7929–4

Typeset by BookEns Ltd, Royston, Herts.
Printed and bound in Great Britain by Antony Rowe, Chippenham, Wiltshire

Contents

An introduction to Alain Badiou's philosophy

Alain Badiou is one of France's foremost living philosophers. Yet recognition of the force and originality of his work in the English-speaking world has been slow to come, perhaps because it is difficult to assimilate his work within the established categories of 'contemporary French philosophy'. However, such recognition is now gathering momentum. No fewer than six translations of his major works, two collections of his essays, and one monograph on his work are currently in press.[1] The first English-language conference devoted to his work was held in May 2002 at Cardiff, a critical introduction to his work has appeared, and three translations of his works – *Ethics, Deleuze,* and *Manifesto for Philosophy* – are already on the shelves.[2]

The present volume aims to provide a brief, accessible introduction to the diversity and power of Badiou's thought, collecting a series of conference papers and essays. The opening text sets the scene, giving a polemical overview of the state of philosophy in relation to the contemporary world. The second chapter gives a general overview, via the categories of ethics and truth, of Badiou's model of fundamental change in the domains of art, love, politics and science – philosophy's four 'conditions'. The following chapters present specific applications of his central conception of philosophy as an exercise of thought conditioned by such changes in art (Chapters 5 and 6 on poetry and cinema), love (Chapter 4 on psychoanalysis), politics (Chapter 3) and science. Since Badiou's work in relation to science is mainly found in the huge tome *L'Etre et l'événement* (*Being and Event*) we chose to sketch the latter's argument in the introduction.[3] Chapters 7 and 8 exemplify a

1

return to one of philosophy's classical roles: the analytical denunciation of ideology, Badiou attacking first the 'war on terrorism' and then the 'death of communism'. The penultimate chapter sets out Badiou's doctrine on philosophy in relation to its conditions, and then the collection closes with an interview with Badiou in which he explains and reconsiders some of his positions.

In our introduction we identify one of the manners in which Badiou's philosophy differs from the contemporary French philosophy known as poststructuralism: its treatment of the question of the subject. We then engage in a long, at times difficult, but necessary exegesis of Badiou's set theory ontology; necessary since it *grounds* his entire doctrine, and not particularly long in relation to its matter; *Being and Event* comprises over 500 pages in the French edition. At every point we have attempted to render the technical details in as clear a fashion as possible, yet without undue distortion.

If the prospective reader wishes to skip over the more abstruse discussions offered in the introduction, he or she should feel absolutely free to do so – for Badiou is still his own best exegete. He effectively tries to speak to those who do not spend their lives in professional institutions, but act and think in ways that usually exceed or are beneath notice. As Badiou himself puts it: 'Philosophy privileges no language, not even the one it is written in.'

Badiou's question

Badiou is neither a poststructuralist nor an analytic philosopher, and for one major reason: there is a question which drives his thought, especially in his magnum opus, *L'Etre et l'événement*. This question is foreign to both poststructuralism and analytic philosophy – in fact not only foreign, but unwelcome. It is this question that governs the peculiarity of Badiou's trajectory and the attendant difficulties of his thought.

In the introduction to *L'Etre et l'événement* Badiou seizes upon an exchange between Jacques-Alain Miller and Jacques Lacan during the famous Seminar XI.[4] Miller, without blinking, asks Lacan, the grand theorist of the barred subject, 'What is your ontology?'[5] For Badiou this is a crucial moment, for it reveals a fundamental difficulty – one that many argue Lacan never solved, even with his loopy 1970s recourses to knot theory. The difficulty is that of reconciling a modern doctrine of the subject (such as that of psychoanalysis) with an ontology. Hence Badiou's guiding question: *How can a modern doctrine of the subject be reconciled with an ontology?*

But what exactly does Badiou understand by a 'modern doctrine of the subject'? Badiou takes it as given that in the contemporary world the subject can no longer be theorized as the self-identical substance that underlies change, nor as the product of reflection, nor as the correlate of an object.[6] This set of negative definitions is all very familiar to a reader of poststructuralism. Surely one could object that poststructuralism has developed a modern doctrine of the subject?

The problem with poststructuralism is that *exactly* the same set of negative definitions serves to delimit its implicit ontology (whether of desire or difference): there are no self-identical substances, there are no stable products of reflection, and since there are no stable objects there can be no correlates of such objects. Thus in poststructuralism there is no distinction between the general field of ontology and a theory of the subject; there is no tension between the being of the subject and being in general.

Where Badiou sees an essential question for modern philosophy, then, poststructuralism sees nothing. For many this lack of distinction between the being of the subject and the being of everything else would appear to be a virtue; the privilege of the rational animal is finally removed in favour of a less anthropocentric ontology. There is, however, a price to be paid for lumping the subject together with whatever else is usually recognized in an ontology. Poststructuralism typically encounters a number of problems in its theory of the subject. Funnily enough, these problems are quite clearly inherited from the very philosophical tradition whose 'death' poststructuralism gleefully proclaims. There was enough life left in the corpse to pass something on – and what it passed on were the two fundamental problems in the thought of the subject.

The first problem is that of *identity*; the second problem, that of *agency*. The mind–body problem derives for the most part from the former, and the free will versus determinism debate from the latter. Poststructuralists have concentrated almost exclusively on a critique of the first problem, arguing that there is no solution to the problem of the identity of the subject because the subject has no substantial identity: the illusion of an underlying identity is produced by the very representational mechanism employed by the subject in its effort to grasp its own identity. The same line of argument is also applied to the identity of any entity – thus including the subject within the domain of a general ontology. For example, in his introduction to a collection of Philippe Lacoue-Labarthe's essays, Derrida identifies the subject with the self-(de)constituting movement of the text; the subject is nothing other than a perpetual movement of translation.[7] This brings the subject within the ambit of his much-maligned but fateful early ontological claim: 'There is no outside-text.' The consequence of this move, of this merger of the subject with a general ontology within the context of a general critique of identity and representation, is the emergence of a problem with the differentiation of subjects. How can one subject be differentiated from another without recourse to some sort of definable identity?

As for agency – philosophy's second fundamental problem in the thought of the subject – the consequence of poststructuralism's almost exclusive concentration on the first problem has been that the critics of poststructuralism have had an easy pitch: all they have had to do is to accuse the poststructuralists of robbing the subject of agency: if there is no self-identical subject, then what is the ground for autonomous rational action? This is what lies behind the infamous jibe that poststructuralism leads down a slippery slope to apoliticism.

When poststructuralists do engage with the problem of agency they again meet with difficulties, and again precisely because they merge their theory of the subject with their general ontology. For example, in his middle period Foucault argued that networks of disciplinary power not only reach into the most intimate spaces of the subject, but actually produce what we call subjects.[8] However, Foucault also said that power produces resistance. His problem then became that of accounting for the source of such resistance. If the subject – right down to its most intimate desires, actions and thoughts – is constituted by power, then how can it be the source of independent resistance? For such a point of agency to exist, Foucault needs some space which has not been completely constituted by power, or a complex doctrine on the relationship between resistance and independence. However, he has neither. In his later work, he deals with this problem by assigning agency to those subjects who resist power by means of an aesthetic project of self-authoring. Again, the source of such privileged agency – why do some subjects shape themselves against the grain and not others? – is not explained.

What does Badiou do when faced with these two fundamental problems of identity and agency? First, Badiou recognizes a distinction between the general domain of ontology and the theory of the subject. He does not merge the one into the other; rather, the *tension* between the two drives his investigations. Second, when it comes to the two problems, Badiou does the exact opposite to the poststructuralists: he defers the problem of identity, leaving a direct treatment of it for the unpublished companion volume to *Being and Event*, while he concentrates on the problem of agency.[9]

For Badiou, the question of agency is not so much a question of how a subject can *initiate* an action in an autonomous manner but rather how a subject *emerges* through an autonomous chain of actions within a changing situation. That is, it is not everyday actions or decisions that provide evidence of agency for Badiou. It is rather those extraordinary decisions and actions which *isolate* an actor from their context, those actions which show that a human can actually be a free agent that supports *new* chains of actions and reactions. For this reason, not every human being is always a subject, yet some human beings *become* subjects; those who act in *fidelity* to a chance encounter with an *event* which disrupts the *situation* they find themselves in.[10]

A subject is born of a human being's decision that something they have *encountered*, which has happened in their situation – however foreign and abnormal – does in fact belong to the situation and thus cannot be overlooked. Badiou marks the disruptive abnormality of such an event by stating that whether it belongs to a situation or not is strictly undecidable on the basis of established knowledge. Moreover, the subject, as born of a decision, is not limited to the recognition of the occurrence of an event, but extends into a prolonged investigation of the consequences of such an event. This investigation is not a passive, scholarly affair; it entails not only the active transformation of the situation in which the event occurs but also the active transformation of the human being. Thus in Badiou's philosophy there is no such thing as a subject without such a process of subjectivization.

For example, when two people fall in love, their 'meeting' – whether that meeting be their first hours together, or the length of their entire courtship – forms an event for them in relation to which they change their lives. This certainly does not mean that their lives are simply going to be the better for it; on the contrary, love may involve debt, alienated friends, and rupture with one's family. The point is that love changes their relation to the world irrevocably. The duration of the lovers' relationship depends upon their fidelity to that event and how they change according to what they discover through their love. In the realm of science the most obvious example of an event is the Copernican revolution, the ensuing subjects being those scientists who worked within its wake contributing to the field we now name 'modern physics'.

The consequence of such a definition of the subject seems to be that only brilliant scientists, modern masters, seasoned militants and committed lovers are admitted into the fold. A little unfair, perhaps? Is Badiou's definition of the subject exclusive or elitist? On the one side, you have human beings, nothing much distinguishing them from animals in their pursuit of their interests, and then, on the other side, you have the new elect, the new elite of faithful subjects. This has a dangerous ring, and one could be forgiven for comparing it at first glance to Mormon doctrine. However – and this is crucial – there is no predestination in Badiou's account. There is nothing other than chance encounters between particular humans and particular events; and subjects *may* be born out of such encounters. There is no higher order which prescribes who will encounter an event and decide to act in relation to it. There is only chance. Furthermore, there is no simple distinction between subjects and humans.[11] Some humans become subjects, but only some of the time, and often they break their fidelity to an event and thus lose their subjecthood.

Thus, Badiou displaces the problem of agency from the level of the human to the level of *being*. That is, his problem is no longer that of how an individual subject initiates a new chain of actions, since for him the subject only emerges in the course of such a chain of actions. His problem is accounting for how an existing situation – given that *being*, for Badiou, is nothing other than multiple situations – can be disrupted and transformed by such a chain of actions. This displacement of the problem of agency allows Badiou to avoid positing some mysterious autonomous agent within each human such as 'free will'. However, the direct and unavoidable consequence of the displacement is that the problem of agency becomes the ancient philosophical problem of how the new occurs in being.

It is no coincidence that Badiou's question – What is the compatibility of a subject with a general ontology? – leads directly to this venerable philosophical problem, since it is this very problem which also underlies Badiou's early work, *Théorie du sujet*.[12] In that work, Badiou's solution was to develop a complex poststructuralist remodelling of the Hegelian dialectic. In *L'Etre et l'événement*, Badiou's solution is simply to assert that 'events happen', events without directly assignable causes which disrupt the order of established situations. *If* decisions are taken by subjects to work out the consequences of such events, *new situations* emerge as a result of their work. Such events do not form part of 'what is', and so they do not fall under the purview of Badiou's general ontology. Thus the relation between the being of the subject and the general domain of Badiou's ontology is a *contingent* relationship, which hinges on the occurrence of an event and the decision of a subject to act in fidelity to that event.

What, then, is this 'general domain' of Badiou's ontology?

Modern ontology: being as multiple multiplicities

As already mentioned, there are two major traditions that enjoy a relation to ontology in late twentieth-century philosophy: the analytic tradition and the post-Heideggerean tradition. The analytic tradition either forecloses ontology in favour of epistemology or reduces ontology to a property of theories.[13] The post-Heideggerean tradition perpetually announces the end of fundamental ontology, while basing this pronouncement on its own fundamental ontology of desire or difference.

Despite his rejection of their conclusions, Badiou does not *simply* dismiss the claims of these traditions. On the contrary, Badiou takes his starting point from both traditions: the concept of 'situation' from Wittgenstein and the idea of the 'ontological difference' from Heidegger. He then forges a new ontology within the furnace of their critiques of ontology.

Heidegger formulates the ontological difference as the difference between Being and beings; that is, the difference between individual beings and the *fact* of their Being, *that they are*. For Badiou the term 'beings' risks substantialization; it is too close to the term 'entity', 'existant' or 'object'. Instead, Badiou proposes the term *situation*, which he defines as a 'presented multiplicity', or as the 'place of taking place' (*EE*, 32). The term 'situation' is prior to any distinction between substances and/or relations and so covers both. Situations include all those flows, properties, aspects, concatenations of events, disparate collective phenomena, bodies, monstrous and virtual, that one might want to examine within an ontology. The concept of 'situation' is also designed to accommodate anything which *is*, regardless of its modality; that is, regardless of whether it is necessary, contingent, possible, actual, potential, or virtual – a whim, a supermarket, a work of art, a dream, a playground fight, a fleet of trucks, a mine, a stock prediction, a game of chess, or a set of waves.

If Aristotle's fundamental ontological claim is 'There are substances', then Badiou's is 'There are situations', or, in other words, 'There are multiple multiplicities'. The key difference between Badiou's claim and that of Aristotle is that for Aristotle each substance is a unity that belongs to a totality – the *cosmos* – which is itself a unity. For Badiou, there is no unified totality that encompasses these multiple multiplicities. Further more, there is no basic or primordial unity to these multiplicities.

It is these two aspects of his ontology which, according to Badiou, guarantee its modernity. For Badiou, the task of modern ontology is to break with classical ontology's fundamental unity of being – both in the latter's individuality and in its totality. Leibniz expressed this belief of classical ontology in the formula: 'What is not *a* being is not a *being.*'[14]

However, breaking with the classical unity of being is no simple task for ontology. The problem is that even if there is no primordial equivalence between unity and being, for Badiou one must still recognize, following Lacan, that *there is some oneness* – 'Il y a de l'un.' That is, although unity is not primordial, there is some kind of effect of unity in the presentation of being.[15] Badiou's solution to this problem is to argue that situations – presented multiplicities – do have unity, but such unity is the result of an operation termed the *count-for-one*. This count is what Badiou terms the situation's *structure*. A structure determines what belongs and does not belong to the situation by counting various multiplicities as *elements* of the situation. An element is a basic unit of a situation. A structure thereby generates unity at the level of *each* element of the situation. It also generates unity at the level of the whole situation by unifying the multiplicity of elements. This is a 'static' definition of a situation: a situation is a presented multiplicity.

Whereas, as we have noted, philosophers have often thought of unity as the fundamental property of Being, for Badiou unity is the *effect* of structuration – and not a ground, origin, or end. The consequence of the unity of situations being the *effect* of an operation is that a multiple that belongs to one situation may also belong to another situation: situations do not have mutually exclusive identities.

The operation of the count-for-one is not performed by some agent separate to the multiplicity of the situation: in classical or even relativist ontologies one can discern such an agent, going under the names of God, History, or Discourse. The distinction between a situation and its structuring count-for-one only holds, strictly speaking, within ontology; the situation is nothing other than this operation of 'counting-for-one'.[16]

If a situation is a counting-for-one, then Badiou also has a dynamic definition of a situation. Once he has both a dynamic as well as a static definition of a situation – the operation of counting-for-one, and unified presented multiplicity – he is able to join his doctrine of multiplicity to a reworking of Heidegger's ontological difference.

Badiou states that the ontological difference stands *between* a situation and the being of that situation; as for Heidegger, this disjointing, in thought, of situations from their being allows ontology to unfold. Unlike Heidegger, however, the being of a situation is not something that only a poetic saying can approach: it is, quite simply and banally, the situation 'before' or rather, *without* the effect of the count-for-one; it is the situation as a non-unified or inconsistent multiplicity. 'After' or *with* the effect of the count-for-one, a situation is a unified or consistent multiplicity.

In order to understand this distinction between an inconsistent multiplicity and a consistent multiplicity, consider the situation of a football team. The particular team we have in mind is a ramshackle set of unruly players each having their own position, strengths and weaknesses; all of whom are *united*, however undisciplined and chaotic their play, by their belonging to the team 'The Cats'.[17] Consider then the same team from the point of view of its being: it is a disparate multiplicity of human bodies, each its own multiplicity of bones, muscles, nerves, arteries, bile and testosterone, each of these sub-elements in turn a multiplicity of cells and so on, which, at the bare level of their brute existence, have nothing to do with that unity termed 'The Cats'. That is, at the level of the being of each element of the team there is nothing which inherently determines that it is *an element* of *this* football team. Thus, at the indifferent level of being, the situation termed 'The Cats' is an inconsistent and non-unified multiplicity. Granted, the proper name 'Cats' does have a certain interpellative power in the Althusserian sense, but it neither resides at nor generates the level of being – for Badiou the word neither murders nor creates the thing, it merely assigns the 'thing' – a multiplicity – a certain identity.

In order to understand how Badiou might equate these inconsistent multiplicities with being, consider stripping something of all of its properties to the extent that even its identity and unity are removed. For many philosophers, parading their commitment to desubstantialization, there would be nothing left after such an operation. However, for Badiou, what would be left would simply be the being of that 'something', and such being could only be *described* as an 'inconsistent multiplicity'. Not even 'formless matter' would be acceptable, since 'matter' would have been one of the general properties we stripped away from our 'something'. Badiou's 'inconsistent multiplicity' is therefore not to be equated with Aristotelian 'prime matter'; its 'actual' status is, moreover, 'undecidable'. Precisely because a situation provokes the question 'What was there *before* all situations?' but provides no possible access to this 'before' that is not irremediably compromised by *post*-situational terminology and operations, it is impossible to speak of in any direct way. With the thought of 'inconsistent multiplicity', thought therefore touches on its own limits; what Badiou calls, following Lacan, its 'real'.

It is at this point that we turn to a discussion of Badiou's use of set theory, by means of which he gives all this rather loose metaphysical talk a solid and precise basis.

Why set theory?

Since Aristotle, ontology has been a privileged sub-discipline of philosophy; otherwise known as the discourse on being. Badiou puts forward a radical thesis: if being is inconsistent multiplicity, then the only suitable discourse for talking about it is no longer philosophy but mathematics. For Badiou, *mathematics is ontology*. Mathematicians, unbeknownst to themselves, do nothing other than continually speak of or write being. This thesis enables Badiou to reformulate the classical language of ontology – being, relations, qualities – in mathematical terms: more specifically, those of set theory because it is one of the foundational disciplines of contemporary mathematics; *any* mathematical proposition can be rewritten in the language of set theory.

In *L'Etre et l'événement*, Badiou sets forth two doctrines to support his adoption of set theory. The first, the doctrine on inconsistent multiplicity, is explained in the previous section. The second is the doctrine on the void. Together, these doctrines serve to bridge the gap between set theory, with its infinity of sets, and Badiou's multiplicities of situations.

Take the first doctrine. If the being of situations is inconsistent multiplicity, what is required of the language of such being? Simply that this language must present multiplicity as inconsistent, that is, as non-unified. To fulfil such a requirement a number of conditions must be met. First, in order to present multiplicity without unity, the multiples presented in this language cannot be multiples of individual things of any kind, since this would be to smuggle back in precisely what is in question – the being of the One. Consequently, these multiples must also be composed of multiples themselves composed of multiples, and so on. Second, ontology cannot present its multiples as belonging to a universe, to one all-inclusive total multiple – for that would be to smuggle back the One at a global level. As such, ontology's multiples must be boundless; they cannot have an upper limit. The third condition is that ontology cannot determine a *single* concept of multiplicity, for that would also unify its multiplicities and, by so doing, unify being.

Set theory is the formal theory of non-unified multiplicities. It meets each of the three conditions outlined above. First, a *set* is a multiple of multiples called *elements*. However, there is no fundamental difference between elements and sets, since every element of a set is itself a set. Second, there is no set of sets; that is, there is no ultimate set which includes all the different types of set found in set theory. Such a set would have to thereby include itself, which is expressly forbidden, on pain of paradox, by one of set theory's axioms, that of foundation.[18] In set theory there is an infinity of infinite types of infinite sets. As for the third condition, there is neither definition nor concept of a set in set theory. What there is in its place is a fundamental *relation* – 'belonging' – as well as a series of variables and logical operators, and nine axioms stating how they may be used together. Sets emerge from operations which follow these rules.

The second doctrine, which Badiou uses to bridge the gap between set theory's infinity of sets and particular non-ontological situations, is his doctrine on 'the void'. Like the doctrine of inconsistent multiplicity, it is also a doctrine about the nature of situations. Badiou argues that, in every situation, there is a being of the 'nothing'. He starts by stating that whatever is recognized as 'something', or as existing, in a situation is counted-for-one in that situation and vice versa. By implication, what is *nothing* in a situation must go uncounted. However, it is not as though there is simply nothing in a situation which is uncounted – both the *operation* of the count-for-one and the *inconsistent multiple* which exists before the count are, by definition, uncountable. Moreover, both are necessary to the existence of a situation or presentation; precisely because they *constitute* a situation as a situation they cannot be presented within the situation itself.[19] As necessary but unpresentable, they constitute what Badiou terms the 'nothing' or the 'void' of a situation.

Badiou states that this void is the 'subtractive suture to being' of a situation (*EE*, 68). The void is the 'suture' of being to presentation because it is the point through which a situation comes to be – the count-for-one – yet by which being – as inconsistent multiplicity – is foreclosed from presentation. The void is 'subtractive' for two reasons. The first is that it is subtracted from presentation and, second, it does not participate in any of the qualities of the situation – although it is proper to the situation, it is as if all of the particularities of the situation are removed or subtracted from it. So, for Badiou, every situation is ultimately founded on a void. This is not Heidegger's *Ab-grund*, nor is it some theological creation *ex nihilo*. The void of a situation is simply what is not there, but what is necessary for anything to be there.

When we turn to set theory, it turns out it makes one initial existential claim, that is, it begins by saying that just one set exists. This particular set is subtracted from the conditions of every other set in set theory: that of having elements. This is the null-set, a multiple of nothing or of the void.[20] On the sole basis of this set, using operations regulated by formal axioms, set theory unfolds an infinity of further sets. Set theory thus weaves its sets out of a 'void', out of what, in any other situation, is the subtractive suture to being of that situation. In other words, we already know that ontology connects to other situations through being the theory of inconsistent multiples. In each and every non-ontological situation, its inconsistent multiplicity is a void. The only possible presentation of a 'void' in set theory is the null-set. Thus, the second way in which set theory connects to situations is that it constructs its inconsistent multiples out of *its* presentation of the void, of the suture to being of every situation.[21]

So much for the *general* connection between situations and set theory's infinite sets. There is also a connection *specific* to each situation: Badiou holds that the structure of each situation can be written as a type of set. That is, leaving all of a situation's properties aside and considering only the basic relations which hold throughout its multiplicity, one can schematize a situation in ontology as a set.

What, then, are sets and how are they written?

Set theory

Sets are made up of elements. The elements of a set have no distinguishing quality save that of *belonging* to it. This is why they are referred to simply as variables – α, β, γ – both when they are elements and when they are themselves considered as sets. The relation of belonging is the basic relation of set theory: it is written α ∈ β; α belongs to β, or, α is an element of the set β. There is another relation in set theory, termed inclusion, which is based entirely on belonging. Sets have 'subsets', that are *included* in the sets. A subset is a grouping of some of a set's elements. Each of a subset's elements must belong to the initial set. Take for example the set δ which consists of the elements α, β, γ. It can be written {α, β, γ}. It has various subsets like {α, β} and {β, γ}. Each subset can itself be given a name, indexed to an arbitrary mark. For example, the latter subset {β, γ}, might be called the subset χ. Its inclusion in δ is written χ ⊂ δ.

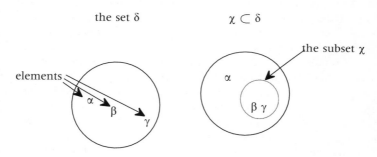

the set δ   χ ⊂ δ

the subset χ

elements

α

β

γ

α

β γ

A set is a *unified* multiplicity: its elements are not indefinite and dispersed; one is able to speak of *a* (single, unified) set. Badiou reads α ∈ β as saying that multiple α is 'counted-for-one' as an element of the set β, or the set β is the 'count-for-one' of all those elements α. Each of those elements α could be counted and grouped and subdivided in different manners, resulting in different sets: there is no restriction on the number of different sets they can belong to. As noted above, this is the great flexibility of set theory – once one strips identity away from multiplicity there is nothing to prevent a multiplicity from belonging to any number of other multiplicities, nothing, that is, save its structure (certain types of sets only admit multiples with certain structures, but more on that later).

If one compares set theory to classical ontologies, indeed even to that of Deleuze, its modernity is immediate. It makes no claims concerning the nature of being, nor concerning the adequation of its categories to being. It makes no attempt to anchor its discourse in necessity through an appeal to some ground, whether etymological, natural or historical. It does not place itself as one linkage within a larger unified machinery such as 'evolution' or 'complexity' or 'chaos'. If there is a grand philosophical claim in Badiou's enterprise, it is not made *within* the discourse of set theory itself but rather holds in the identification of set theory *as* ontology. The basis of set theory is simply a set of axioms. The necessity of these axioms has been tested rather than declared insofar as all operations made on their basis must have logically consistent results. These results have been tested through a century of work within set theory. Nine axioms regulate the operations and the existences which weave the tissue of set theory's universe.

For Badiou these axioms constitute a *decision* in thought, a starting point. The axioms themselves, of course, are not pure historical beginnings since they are the result of a series of reformulations made over the first few decades of set theory: these reformulations were designed to prevent the occurrence of logical inconsistency within the domain of set theory. Rather, they mark the beginning of something new in scientific thought inasmuch as, for example, it was not possible to conceive of two different types of infinity, one larger than the other, before Cantor's pioneering work in set theory.

Set theory itself comes in a number of varieties: for example, there are foundational and anti-foundational types, with varying numbers and types of axioms. Badiou's own choice is to plump for the orthodox version of Zermelo-Fraenkel set theory, with its nine axioms. These are generally called: Extensionality, Separation, Power-Set, Union, Empty Set, Infinity, Foundation, Replacement and Choice. An explanation of all nine of these axioms would exceed the range of this presentation, but a quick sketch of five of the nine axioms should shed some light on how the universe of set theory unfolds.

The first concerns identity and difference, the axiom of extension: If every element γ of a set α is also an element of a set β and the inverse is true, then the sets α and β are indistinguishable and therefore identical. Consequently, in set theory ontology, the regime of identity and difference is founded upon extension, not quality. That is, every difference is localized in a point: for two sets to be different, at least one element of one of the sets must not belong to the other.

The next three 'constructive' axioms allow the construction of a new set on the basis of an already existing set. The axiom of separation states: 'If there exists a set α, then there exists a subset β of α, all of whose elements γ satisfy the formula F.' It enables a set defined by a formula to be separated out from an initial set. If one gives values to the variables one could then, for example, separate out the subset, β, of all green apples from the set of apples, α ('green apples' being the formula in this example).

The power-set axiom states that all of the subsets of an initial set grouped together form another set termed the power-set. Take for example the set {α, β, χ}. Its three elements can be grouped into the following subsets: {α}, {β}, {χ}, {α, β}, {α, χ}, and {β, χ}, to which must be added both what is termed the 'maximal' subset {α, β, χ}, and, by virtue of a rule explained later, the null-set {∅}. The power-set of {α, β, χ} is thus:

$$\{\{\alpha\}, \{\beta\}, \{\chi\}, \{\alpha, \beta\}, \{\alpha, \chi\}, \{\beta, \chi\}, \{\alpha, \beta, \chi\} \{\varnothing\}\}.$$

It is important to note that the power-set of any set is always demonstrably larger than the initial set. This means one can always generate larger sets out of any existing set.

The axiom of union states that all of the elements, δ, of the elements, γ, of an initial set, α, themselves form another set β termed the union-set. The new set β is thus the union-set of the initial set α, conventionally written ∪α. It shows that sets are homogeneously multiple when decomposed.

All the axioms listed so far presume the existence of at least one set but they do not themselves establish the existence of sets. The axiom of the null-set, on the other hand, does. It forms set theory's first ontological commitment. It states that there exists a null-set, an empty set to which no elements belong – ∅. This null-set is the initial point of existence from which all the other sets of set theory are unfolded using the constructive axioms. For example, from ∅, by the operations prescribed by the axiom of the power-set, one can demonstrate the existence of its power-set {∅}, and then by repeating the operation, further sets can be unfolded such as {∅, {∅}} and {∅, {∅}, {∅, {∅}}}. It is just such unfolding which constitutes the infinity of sets.

Each of these axioms has profound consequences for philosophical problems, once one allows that set theory is ontology. In order to use set theory to address philosophical problems Badiou makes a distinction between ontology proper, that is, the formal language of set theory, and the discourse of meta-ontology, that is, a translation of set theory's axioms and theorems into philosophical terms. Thus for every set-theoretical term, there is an equivalent in the discourse of philosophy. For example, a set is spoken of in meta-ontology as a 'multiplicity', a 'situation' or a 'presentation'.

One of the traditional philosophical problems to which set theory responds is that of the relationship between being and language. According to Badiou, this relationship is concentrated in the way set theory ties the existence of sets together with their definitions. In one of the first formulations of set theory, that of Gottlieb Frege, a set is defined as 'the extension of a concept'. This means that for any well-formed formula in a first order logic which defines a concept, a set of elements exists, each of which satisfies the formula.[22] That is, there can be no sets, and thus nothing in existence, for which there is no concept: every existing set corresponds to a concept. Or, whenever one has a defined concept, one can directly deduce the existence of a corresponding multiple. Thus, the relationship between language and being is one of exact correspondence.

However, Frege's definition of sets – and, by implication, his articulation of the relationship between language and being – met with a problem. In 1902, Bertrand Russell discovered a well-formed formula to which no existent set could correspond without introducing contradiction into set theory.[23] The formula is 'the set of all sets which are not members of themselves'. The contradiction ensues when one asks whether the set of elements which satisfies this formula belongs to itself or not. If it does belong to itself then, by definition, it does not, and if it does not belong to itself, then it does. This contradiction ruins the consistency of the formal language in which the formula is made. The consequence of the paradox is that it is not true that for every well-formed formula a corresponding multiple exists.

In order to avoid Russell's paradox, the axiom of separation was developed. It proposes another relationship between the existence of multiples and well-formed formulas. Frege's definition of that relationship runs as follows:

$$(\exists \beta) \ (\forall \alpha) \ [F(\alpha) \ \rightarrow \ (\alpha \in \beta)].$$

This proposition reads: 'There exists a set β such that every term α which satisfies the formula F is an element of that set.' The axiom of separation on the other hand looks like this:

$$(\forall \alpha) \ (\exists \beta) \ (\forall \gamma) \ [(\ (\gamma \in \alpha) \ \& \ F(\gamma)) \ \rightarrow \ (\gamma \in \beta)].$$

It reads: 'If there exists a set α, then there exists a subset β of α, all of whose elements γ satisfy the formula F.' The essential difference between Frege's definition and the axiom of separation is that the former directly proposes an existence while the latter is *conditional* upon there already being a set in existence, α. The axiom of separation says that *if* there is a set already in existence, then one can *separate out* one of its subsets, β, whose elements validate the formula F. Say for example that the formula F is the property 'rotten' and one wants to make the judgement 'Some apples are rotten.' Via the axiom of separation, from the *supposed* existence of the set of all apples, one could separate out the subset of rotten apples.

The relationship between being and language implied by the axiom of separation is therefore not one of an exact fit, but rather one in which language causes 'a split or division in existence' (*EE*, 58). The conclusion Badiou thus draws from set theory for the traditional philosophical problem of the relationship between language and being is that, although language bestows identity on being, being is in excess of language. This is quite clearly a materialist thesis as befits Badiou's Marxist heritage. In meta-ontological terms, the axiom of separation states that an *undefined* existence must always be assumed in any definition of a type of multiple. In short, the very conditions of the inscription of existence in language require that existence be in excess of what the inscriptions define as existing.

So, what is the general result of Badiou's adoption of set theory as the language of being? Quite simply that it has nothing to say about beings themselves – this is the province of other discourses such as physics, anthropology and literature. This is one reason why Badiou terms set theory a *subtractive* ontology: it speaks of beings without reference to their attributes or their identity; it is as if the beings ontology speaks of have had all their qualities subtracted from them. As a result, unlike Plato and Aristotle's ontologies, there is neither cosmos nor phenomena, neither cause nor substance. Set theory ontology does not propose a description of 'the furniture of the world', nor does it concern itself with 'carving reality at the joints'. Its own ontological claim simply amounts to saying there is a multiplicity of multiplicities. Furthermore, set theory ontology is indifferent to the existence or non-existence of particular situations such as 'the world' or 'you, the reader': Badiou writes: 'we are attempting to think multiple-presentation *regardless of* time (which is founded by intervention), and space (which is a singular construction, relative to certain types of presentation)' (*EE*, 293). What set theory ontology does, in lieu of presenting 'what there is', is present the ontological schemas of any ontological claim; that is, it presents the structure of what any situation *says exists*.

Ontological schemas of different situations

Although set theory ontology does not recognize the infinite differentiations of concrete situations, it does recognize a number of differences in the *structure* of situations. This allows it to schematize different concrete situations. According to Badiou's meta-ontology, there are three basic structures which are found underpinning every existent situation. To understand the differentiation of these structures it is necessary to return to the axiom of the power-set and its meta-ontological equivalents.

The axiom of the power-set says that there is a set of all the subsets of an initial set, termed the power-set. In meta-ontological terms, the power-set is the *state* of a situation. This means that every multiple already counted as one, is counted again at the level of its sub-multiples: the state is thus a *second* count-for-one. Or, according to another of Badiou's meta-ontological translations, if a set schematizes a presentation, then its power-set schematizes the representation of that presentation.[24] The state is made up of all the possible regroupings of the elements of a situation; as such it is the structure which underlies any representational or grouping mechanism in any situation. We should note that as such the term 'state' includes but is in no way reducible to the position of a government and its administration in a political situation.

Badiou distinguishes three types of situation: natural, historical and neutral. What makes them different at a structural level are the types of multiple which compose them. There are three types of multiple: *normal* multiples, which are both presented by the situation and represented by its state (they are counted-for-one twice); *excrescent* multiples, which are only represented by the state; and *singular* multiples, which only occur at the level of presentation, and which escape the effect of the second count-for-one.

Natural situations are defined as having no singular multiples – all of their multiples are either normal or excrescent, and each normal element in turn has normal elements (*EE*, 146). Neutral situations are defined as having a mix of singular, normal and excrescent multiples.[25] Historical situations are defined by their having at least one 'evental-site'; a sub-type of singular multiple.[26] In set theory terms, a singular multiple is an element of a set, but not one of its subsets. Since each of a set's subsets is made entirely of elements that already belong to the initial set, the definition of a singular multiple is that, first, it is an element of an initial set, and, second, some of its own elements in turn do not belong to the initial set. It is these foreign elements which are responsible for the singularity of a singular multiple. An *eventaI-site* is an extreme variety of a singular multiple: none of an evental-site's elements also belong to the initial set. Leaving normal situations aside, let us turn to examples of natural and historical situations.

Take, for an example of a natural situation, the ecosystem of a pond. The multiples which it presents include individual fish, tadpoles, reeds and stones. Each of these elements is also represented at the level of the state of the situation, which Badiou also qualifies as the level of the *knowledges* of a situation – these elements are *known* elements of the situation. Each element of an ecosystem is also one of the ecosystem's subsets, because each of their elements also belong, in turn, to the ecosystem; for example each fish's eating and breeding habits belong to the ecosystem as well as to each fish. These elements are thus normal multiples. If one examines such a situation, it contains no singular terms: nothing is presented which is not also represented. The test of whether a situation is natural or not is whether there is any element of the situation whose content is not also part of the situation – in ecology, every element of a system, at whatever level of size or effect, is interconnected. The situation of the ecosystem of a pond is thus a natural situation.

Take, by contrast, as an example of a historical situation, a collection of possible answers to the nationalist concern of *what it is to be Australian*. Some of the multiples presented in this situation would be *individual* stories about bronzed lifesavers, Anzac soldiers, larrikins, whinging poms, wowsers, convicts, explorers, bushrangers and squatters. One would also find Don Bradman and the Eureka Stockade belonging to such a collection. In the twenty-first century, this situation's elements would also comprise individual stories about the Italian-Australians, the Irish-Australians, the Chinese-Australians, the Greek-Australians, the Turkish-Australians, and so on. At the level of the state of the situation one has submultiples such as hedonism, mateship, equality understood as sameness, the imperatives 'fair go!' and 'she'll be right mate!', anti-British sentiment, distrust of authority, the privileging of know-how over theory, Protestantism, and Catholicism, etc.

From both socio-economic and cultural perspectives, immigrant groups are both presented and re-presented. Their contribution to 'what it is to be Australian' is both known and knowable. For this reason we would argue that none of the presented 'immigrant' multiples are *singular* multiples. On the other hand, constitutively resistant to Anglo-Saxon dreams of assimilation, the multiple 'aboriginals' forms an evental-site; its contents remain unknown. Of course, within other situations such as cultural, sociological and bureaucratic assessments of Australia, 'aboriginals' are re-presented. However, these specialized discourses are not in the position of furnishing answers to the nationalist question 'What is it to be Australian?' The multiple 'aboriginals' forms an evental-site because the sovereignty of Australia, the 'immigrant nation', was *founded* upon the dispossession of indigenous peoples. Their relation to this particular piece of land was crucially not recognized at the very beginning of this entity termed 'Australia'. Any representation of the content of the multiple 'aboriginals' with reference to what it is to be Australian, would thus cause the unity of the situation to dissolve – in a sense, it would entail *the dissolution of 'Australia' itself*. It is this *constitutive irrepresentability* at the heart of Australian nationalism that makes it a *historical* situation.

Badiou uses this division between natural and historical situations to return to his basic question: How does the new happen in being? In our mythical, pollution-free pond, though there may be generation after generation of 'new' baby fish, nothing really changes: barring another natural catastrophe the ecosystem will remain in a state of homeostasis. In natural situations Ecclesiastes' proverb holds true: there is nothing new under the sun. In historical situations things are quite different. To return to our example of Australian nationalism, the inherent instability of the situation (it harbouring an unknowable evental-site in its midst) renders it susceptible to wholesale political transformation.

However, the existence of an evental-site in a situation does not guarantee that change will occur. For that something extra is required, a 'supplement' as Badiou says, which is an *event*. We are not talking about any ordinary event here, like a birthday or Australia beating France in rugby, but rather of a totally disruptive occurrence which has no place in the scheme of things as they currently are. Who will say what this event has been or will be for Australian nationalism – was it the erection by Aboriginal activists of a tent embassy opposite the National Parliament in 1972? The occurrence of an event is completely unpredictable.[27] There is no meta-situation – 'History' – which would programme the occurrence of events in various selected situations.

The precariousness of historical change extends further: not only must an event occur at the evental-site of a situation, but someone must recognize and name that event as an event whose implications concern the nature of the entire situation. Thus it is quite possible that an event occur in a situation but that nothing changes because nobody recognizes the event's importance for the situation. This initial naming of the event as an event, this decision that it has transformational consequences for the entirety of a situation, is what Badiou terms an 'intervention'. The intervention is the first moment of a process of fundamental change that Badiou terms a 'fidelity', or a 'generic truth procedure'. A generic truth procedure is basically a praxis consisting of a series of enquiries into the situation made by militants who act in fidelity to the event. The object of these enquiries is to work out how to transform the situation in line with what is revealed by the event's belonging to the situation. For example, within the situation of art in the early twentieth century, certain artists launched an enquiry into the nature of sculpture once Picasso's cubist paintings had been recognized as 'art'. The procedure made up of such enquiries is termed a 'truth procedure' because it unfolds a new multiple: the 'truth' of the previous situation. Here Badiou draws upon – and displaces – Heidegger's conception of truth as the presentation of being. The new entity is a truth inasmuch as it presents the *multiple-being* of the previous situation, stripped bare of any predicates, of any identity.

For example, take an art critic in the early twentieth century who has just recognized that a cubist painting can, indeed, be called 'art'. If he was called upon to make a predicative definition of the contemporary situation of art – that is, if someone asked him 'What is art?' – he would have found it impossible to respond – at that very moment, for him, the disruptive event we now call 'cubism' was laying bare the situation of art as a pure multiplicity of colours, forms, materials, proper names, titles and spaces *with no fixed contours*. In fact, the common accusation that contemporary art is gratuitous, indeterminate, and as such could be 'anything whatsoever' with a label slapped on it stuck in a gallery; this very accusation actually unknowingly strikes upon the very nature of a new multiple: it is 'anything whatsoever' with regard to established knowledge.

To understand how a new multiple – such as 'modern art' – can both exist, and be stripped bare of any predicates (as such being globally indescribable or 'anything whatsoever') we must turn back to Badiou's use of set theory.

Generic sets and processes of transformation

In order to think about processes of fundamental change *within* his ontology Badiou had to work out how a multiple, a set, can be new. It is at this point that Badiou introduces the centrepiece of his work – what he calls 'the generic' or 'indiscernibility'. This is at once an extremely difficult concept, based on the most innovative mathematical procedures, yet also intuitively graspable. Badiou takes this concept from the work of Paul Cohen, an American mathematician who invented the 'generic' set in 1963.[28]

The first point to work out is what the reference point could be *within ontology* for such novelty. Especially since set theory ontology appears to be a static, flat discourse, with no recognition of the supposed universality of the situations of 'time' and 'history'. The reference point turns out to be *language*. In set theory, one can have 'models' of set theory which are interpretations that flesh out the bare bones of sets and elements by giving values to the variables (such as γ = green apples in the example used above). A model of set theory has its own language in which various formulas express certain properties such as 'green'. The model itself, as a structured multiplicity, can be treated itself as a set. Cohen takes as his starting point what he terms a 'ground model' of set theory. Badiou takes this model as the schema of a historical situation. Each subset of this model satisfies a property which can be expressed in the language used in the model. That is, every multiple found in the model can be discerned using the tools of language. A generic set, on the other hand, is a subset that is 'new' insofar as it cannot be discerned by that language. For every property that one formulates, even the most general such as 'this apple and this apple and this apple . . .', the generic set has *at least one* element which does not share that property. This makes sense intuitively: when someone tries to tell you about a new experience, whether it be meeting a person or seeing a work of art, they have a lot of trouble describing it accurately and, every time you try to help them by suggesting that it might be a bit like the person *x* or the film *y*, they say, 'No, no, it's not like that!' For every property or concept you come up with to describe this new thing, there is something in that new thing which does not quite fit. This is all very well, but having a set which one 'can't quite describe' sounds a bit vague for set theory. The innovation of Paul Cohen's work lay in his discovery of a method of describing such a multiple without betraying its *indiscernibility*.[29]

But what about the process of this new multiple coming into being? How does a generic set provide the ontological schema of processes of radical change in political, scientific, artistic, and amorous situations? Badiou holds that the ground model schematizes an established historical situation before an event arrives. One can define a concept of a generic subset within such a situation but one cannot know that it exists – precisely because it is one of those 'excrescent' multiples noted above (which are not presented at the level of belonging to a situation). The generic subset is only present at the level of inclusion, and, unlike all the other subsets, it cannot be known via its properties. To show that a generic set actually exists, Cohen develops a procedure whereby one adds it to the existing ground model as a type of supplement, thereby forming a new set. Within this new set, the generic multiple will exist at the level of belonging, or in meta-ontological terms, presentation. The new supplemented set provides the ontological schema of a historical situation which has undergone wholesale change.

Furthermore, Cohen developed a method of making finite descriptions of this new supplemented set using only the resources of the initial set. Cohen termed this procedure 'forcing' and Badiou adopts it as an ontological model of the numerous practical enquiries that subjects who act in fidelity to an event make while they are attempting to bring about the change entailed by the event. That is, although, say, an activist working towards justice for the indigenous peoples in Australia will not know what overall shape justice will take, they will be able to predict certain of its features and some of their predictions may be verified early on in the process of change. For example, a particular experiment in public health practices in indigenous communities may reveal itself to be part of the movement towards justice due to its sensitivity to issues of self-determination and cultural difference.

For Badiou, the actual work which carries out the wholesale change of a historical situation – in his terms, the fidelity practised by subjects to an event – consists of such experiments; finite enquiries into the nature of the event, using an invented idiom to approximate what is discovered through such enquiries. Historically, one can understand this concept of fidelity as a remodelling of the Marxist concept of praxis, subtracting the latter from the encompassing unities of historical determinism, revolutionary theory and the Party line. What results from such subtractions is a praxis made up of a hazardous series of bets, bets on the nature of the situation to come. Many of these bets will fall wide of the mark, but those that hit the target will help construct the new situation.

Of course, Badiou recognizes that the number of shapes a fidelity can take, especially in domains as different as art, politics, science and love, is infinite; and further, that a number of different fidelities may be developed in the same situation to the same event – for example, both Pierre Boulez and John Cage developed their music in fidelity to the event of Schoenberg's invention of the twelve-tone series, but in very different directions. Yet Badiou's general claim is that in *each* case of a fidelity it is a matter of the new coming into being, and in set theory ontology the only way to schematize that process is through Paul Cohen's concepts of the generic set and forcing. Thus, however particular – and indeed, however precarious – a decolonization process within a colonialist political situation, at the level of the structure of its multiplicity, it is a generic set. The relation this process entertains with the established colonialist situation is not one of pure exteriority (romanticism) nor of subsumption (realism), but that of *indiscernibility*. That is, none of the categories employed by colonialist discourses serve to discern its nature.

Hence the indiscernibility of a generic truth procedure grounds both its singularity and its sovereignty, insofar as it is subtracted from and thus independent of any known entity in the situation, such as 'parliamentary democracy', 'mining interests', 'the proletariat', or 'the native'.

But within the debates around post-colonialism, the romantics and the realists will always have one last objection to an argument such as ours: that there is an exception to the rule, since the categories of one colonialist discourse in particular seem to serve quite well for discerning the nature of a decolonization process, the latest categories of European philosophy, those of Alain Badiou's set theory ontology. However, this would be to miss the point entirely. Ontology does not discern the *nature* of any situation, much less that of a particular fidelity. Ontology only speaks of the *structure* of multiplicity: it has nothing to say about the qualities or identity of any concrete situation. For Badiou such would be the province of other discourses, practical or theoretical. This is the first guard against imperialism built into Badiou's philosophy – the indifference of ontology towards the concrete.

The second guard lies in Badiou's refusal of any transitivity between ontology and politics. As a good materialist, he recognizes the autonomy of material processes and argues that the names philosophy comes up with to reflect particular political transformations *are not* and *cannot* be identical to those names that are thrown up by the actual process of transformation within a political situation. The task of philosophy is not to predict nor determine the shape of justice, or of modern art, or even the form a unified field theory might take. Philosophy's task is to reflect and learn from those transformations happening in contemporary historical situations; to the point where it develops what Badiou terms a 'space of *compossibility*' for all contemporary fidelities. The relationship between philosophy and politics – as with art, science and love – is thus one of conditioning or dependence. Philosophy is no longer sovereign. It is as if philosophy has finally heard that cry addressed to it for decades, a cry voiced by so many artists, scientists, activists and lovers whose activities it has deafly appropriated from on high, the cry 'SHUT UP AND LISTEN!!!'

And even if Badiou's conception of philosophy maintains a strict separation between the practice of philosophy and the diverse practices of art, politics, science and love, it does have one practical consequence. Quite simply, if you want to do politics, go become an activist, go decide what event has happened in your political situation. If you want to do philosophy, try to think the compossibility of contemporary events in each of the four domains of art, politics, science and love (and, of course, read all of *Being and Event* once it's published). Just don't confuse the two.

A note on notes

Following Badiou's practice, we do not reference texts he mentions, trusting the readers' own curiosity to guide them. Admittedly, it is a rather abrupt gesture. It does not place thought under the sign of the demand for knowledge but simply under that of desire.

Notes

1   The following titles by Alain Badiou are currently in press or forthcoming: *Being and Event*, trans. Oliver Feltham (London: Continuum Books, forthcoming); *Theoretical Writings*, trans. and ed. Alberto Toscano and Ray Brassier (London: Continuum Books, 2003); *Handbook of Inaesthetics*, trans. A. Toscano (Stanford, CA: Stanford University Press, 2003); *St. Paul: The Foundation of Universalism*, trans. R. Brassier (Stanford, CA: Stanford University Press, 2003); *On Beckett*, ed. and trans. Nina Power and A. Toscano with Bruno Bosteels (Manchester: Clinamen, 2003); *The Century/Le Siècle*, trans. A.

Toscano with responses by A. Toscano and Slavoj Zizek (Paris/London: Seuil/ Verso, 2003). Badiou's *Abrégé de Métapolitique* (Paris: Seuil, 1998), translated by Jason Barker, is forthcoming from Verso. See also Peter Hallward, *Subject to Truth: An Introduction to the Philosophy of Alain Badiou* (Minneapolis: University of Minnesota Press, forthcoming) and P. Hallward (ed.), *Think Again: Alain Badiou and the Future of Philosophy* (London: Continuum Books, forthcoming).

2　See J. Barker, *Alain Badiou: A Critical Introduction* (London: Pluto Press, 2002); A. Badiou, *Ethics: An Essay on the Understanding of Evil*, trans. Peter Hallward (London: Verso, 2001); A. Badiou, *Gilles Deleuze: The Clamor of Being*, trans. Louise Burchill (Minneapolis: University of Minnesota Press, 2000); A. Badiou, *Manifesto for Philosophy*, trans. Norman Madarasz (Albany, NY: SUNY Press, 1999).

3　A. Badiou, *L'Etre et l'événement* (Paris: Editions du Seuil, 1988). All further references will appear as page numbers in brackets in the body of the text.

4　Jacques Lacan was a French psychoanalyst famous for his fusion of Freud, Saussurean linguistics, structuralist anthropology, French psychiatry and mathematics into one continually evolving and powerful theory of the subject. Jacques-Alain Miller subsequently became Lacan's son-in-law, executor of his estate, head of one of the largest Lacanian schools of psychoanalysis, and one of Lacan's premier commentators.

5　Ontology is the philosophical discourse defined by Aristotle as the science of being qua being. Historically it has treated such questions as 'What is being?' and 'Why is there something rather than nothing?'

6　For a particularly dense and concentrated elaboration of Badiou's theory of the subject see 'A finally objectless subject', in the anthology *Who Comes After the Subject?* ed. E. Cadava (London: Routledge, 1991).

7　Jacques Derrida, 'Desistance', in Philippe Lacoue-Labarthe, *Typography, Mimesis, Politics, Philosophy*, ed. C. Fynsk (Cambridge, MA: Harvard University Press, 1989).

8　See, for instance, M. Foucault, *Power/Knowledge: Selected Interviews and Other Writings 1972–1977*, ed. C. Gordon, trans. C. Gordon *et al.* (New York: Pantheon, 1980).

9　A. Badiou, *Logiques des mondes* (Paris: Seuil, forthcoming). Insofar as Badiou's concept of a generic multiple, which makes up the 'stuff' of his faithful subjects, delivers a rigorous definition of singularity, one could argue that the classical problem of the identity of subjects, or that of their differentiation, is indirectly treated inasmuch as the generic multiple is strictly differentiated from every predicate. See 'Generic sets and processes of transformation', pp. 22–25.

10　'Fidelity', 'event', and 'situation' are all technical terms of Badiou's ontology and their meaning will be explained in what follows; however, the reader's intuitive sense of these words can be trusted to provide an initial approximation.

11 At this point we should note an important complication of Badiou's theory of the subject; Badiou also terms 'subject' the actual individual theorems which make up modern physics. Similarly in the domain of art he terms 'subject' particular musical works rather than their composers. This shift simply reinforces his separation between the human as an individual animal, and the human acting as subject, that is as a point of risk, invention and decision.

12 A. Badiou, *Théorie du sujet* (Paris: Seuil, 1981).

13 See Willard V. O. Quine, 'Ontological relativity', in *Ontological Relativity and Other Essays* (New York: Columbia University Press, 1969).

14 G. W. Leibniz, 'Letter to Arnauld April 30 1687', in *Philosophical Writings*, trans. J. M. Morris (London: Dent & Sons, 1934), 72.

15 According to Badiou this was also Kant's problem in the first critique insofar as the latter did not grant immediate unity either to the thing itself or to the sensuous manifold, yet attempted to account for the apparent unity of experience.

16 See the interview included in this volume.

17 We would like to thank our colleague Amelia Smith for this example.

18 This axiom was introduced in order to deal with a paradox that appeared early in the development of set theory. Russell's paradox emerges on the basis of sets being able to be members of themselves. It is more familiar in the paradox of the barber who shaves all the men in the village who don't shave themselves: who shaves the barber? We return to this paradox below.

19 Students of philosophy may be reminded of the status of Kant's *Ding-an-sich* and of transcendental apperception in the first *Critique*.

20 In French, *l'ensemble-vide*. In Badiou's text this harmonizes at a terminological level with the French for 'the void of a situation': *le vide de la situation*.

21 The doctrine on inconsistent multiplicity is prior, in the order of argument, to the doctrine on the void of situations – because to accept that set theory's null-set presents the nothing of situations, one must already have accepted that sets present the being of situations.

22 A first order logic consists of a series of signs: existential and universal quantifiers, variables, properties and logical connectors; disjunction, conjunction, implication, negation and equivalence. Properties are never found in the position of variables, that is, first order logic does not express properties of properties: that is the province of second order logic.

23 See B. Russell, 'Letter to Frege', in J. Van Heijenoort (ed.), *From Frege to Gödel: A Source Book in Mathematical Logic* (Cambridge, MA: Harvard University Press, 1967), 124.

24 We should note that if this meta-ontological translation is legitimate, the superior size and complexity of the power-set, with regard to its initial set, has fundamental consequences for the classical philosophical problem of the relationship between presentation and representation (and thus for any

practice based on the critique of representations), as it does for the classical political problem of the relation between the state and the people.

25 Due to the excess of inclusion over belonging – the superior size of a set's power-set compared to itself – every situation has excrescent multiples.

26 'Evental-site' is a neologism that has been coined in order to translate Badiou's *site événementiel*. 'Event-site' is not appropriate, because it suggests that the site is defined by the occurrence of an event, whereas in Badiou's conception, there is no guarantee that an event *will* occur at a *site événementiel*, the sole guarantee being that if an event does occur in the situation it will do so at that particular point of the latter termed the evental-site.

27 This is precisely how Badiou breaks with historical determinisms.

28 The reference for the mathematicians is P. Cohen, *Set Theory and the Continuum Hypothesis* (New York: W.A. Benjamin, 1966).

29 See Meditations 34 and 35 of *L'Etre et l'événement* for a full explanation of Cohen's method.

1
Philosophy and desire

This philosophical investigation begins under the banner of poetry; thus recalling the ancient tie between poetry and philosophy.[1]

Rimbaud employs a strange expression: 'les révoltes logiques', 'logical revolts'. Philosophy is something like a 'logical revolt'. Philosophy pits thought against injustice, against the defective state of the world and of life. Yet it pits thought against injustice in a movement which conserves and defends argument and reason, and which ultimately proposes a new logic.

Mallarmé states: 'All thought begets a throw of the dice.' It seems to me that this enigmatic formula also designates philosophy, because philosophy proposes to think the universal – that which is true for all thinking – yet it does so on the basis of a commitment in which chance always plays a role, a commitment which is also a risk or a wager.

The four-dimensional desire of philosophy

These two poetic formulas capture the desire of philosophy, for at base the desire of philosophy implies a dimension of *revolt*: there is no philosophy without the discontent of thinking in its confrontation with the world as it is. Yet the desire of philosophy also includes *logic*; that is, a belief in the power of argument and reason. Furthermore, the desire of philosophy involves *universality*: philosophy addresses all humans as thinking beings since it supposes that all humans think. Finally, philosophy takes *risks*: thinking is always a decision which supports independent points of view. The desire of philosophy thus has four dimensions: revolt, logic, universality and risk.

I think that the contemporary world, our world, the world that we strive to think and transform, exerts an intense pressure upon these four dimensions of the desire of philosophy; such that all four dimensions, faced by the world, find themselves in a difficult and dark passage in which the destiny and even the very existence of philosophy is at stake.

To begin with, as far as the dimension of revolt is concerned, this world, our world, the 'Western' world (with as many inverted commas as you want), does not engage in thought as revolt, and for two reasons. First, this world already decrees itself free, it presents itself as 'the free world' – this is the very name it gives itself, an 'isle' of liberty on a planet otherwise reduced to slavery or devastation. Yet, at the same time – and this is the second reason – this world, our world, standardizes and commercializes the stakes of such freedom. It submits them to monetary uniformity, and with such success that our world no longer has to revolt to be free since it guarantees us freedom. However, it does not guarantee us the free use of this freedom, since such use is in reality already coded, orientated and channelled by the infinite glitter of merchandise. This is why this world exerts an intense pressure against the very idea that thinking can be insubordination or revolt.

Our world also exerts a strong pressure on the dimension of logic; essentially because the world is submitted to the profoundly illogical regime of communication. Communication transmits a universe made up of disconnected images, remarks, statements and commentaries whose accepted principle is incoherence. Day after day communication undoes all relations and all principles, in an untenable juxtaposition that dissolves every relation between the elements it sweeps along in its flow. And what is perhaps even more distressing is that mass communication presents the world to us as a spectacle devoid of memory, a spectacle in which new images and new remarks cover, erase and consign to oblivion the very images and remarks that have just been shown and said. The logic which is specifically undone there is the logic of time. It is these processes of communication which exert pressure on the resoluteness of thinking's fidelity to logic; proposing to thought in the latter's place a type of imaginary dissemination.

As for the universal dimension of the desire of philosophy, our world is no longer suited to it because the world is essentially a specialized and fragmentary world; fragmented in response to the demands of the innumerable ramifications of the technical configuration of things, of the apparatuses of production, of the distribution of salaries, of the diversity of functions and skills. And the requirements of this specialization and this fragmentation make it difficult to perceive what might be transversal or universal; that is, what might be valid for all thinking.

Finally, we have the dimension of risk. Our world does not favour risky commitments or risky decisions, because it is a world in which nobody has the means any more to submit their existence to the perils of chance. Existence requires more and more elaborate calculation. Life is devoted to calculating security, and this obsession with calculating security is contrary to the Mallarméan hypothesis that thought begets a throw of the dice, because in such a world there is infinitely too much risk in a throw of the dice.

The desire for philosophy thus encounters four principal obstacles in the world. These are: the reign of merchandise, the reign of communication, the need for technical specialization and the necessity for realistic calculations of security. How can philosophy take on this challenge? Is philosophy capable of such a challenge? The answer must be sought in the state of contemporary philosophy.

The present state of philosophy

What are the principal global tendencies in contemporary philosophy if we consider it from a bird's eye point of view?

I think it can be said that three principal orientations can be distinguished in philosophy today. These orientations correspond, in some measure, to three geographical locations. I will first name and then describe them. The first can be called the hermeneutic orientation, which historically goes back to German romanticism. The best-known names attached to this orientation are Heidegger and Gadamer, and its historical site was originally German. Then there is the analytic orientation, originating with the Vienna Circle. The principal names connected to it are those of Wittgenstein and Carnap. Despite its Austrian origin, it now dominates English and American academic philosophy. Finally, we have what can be called the postmodern orientation, which in fact borrows from the other two. It is without doubt the most active in France, and includes thinkers as different as Jacques Derrida and Jean-François Lyotard. It is equally very active in Spain, Italy and Latin America.

A hermeneutic orientation, an analytic orientation, and a postmodern orientation: there are, of course, innumerable intersections, mixtures and networks of circulation between the three, but together they form the most global and descriptive geography possible of contemporary philosophy. What then interests us is how each orientation designates or identifies philosophy.

The hermeneutic orientation assigns philosophy the aim of deciphering the meaning of Being, the meaning of Being-in-the-world, and its central concept is that of *interpretation*. There are statements, acts, writings, and configurations whose meaning is obscure, latent, hidden or forgotten. Philosophy must be provided with a method of interpretation that will serve to clarify this obscurity, and bring forth from it an authentic meaning, a meaning which would be a figure of our destiny in relation to the destiny of being itself. The fundamental opposition for hermeneutic philosophy is that of the closed and the open. In what is given, in the immediate world, there is something dissimulated and closed. The aim of interpretation is to undo this closure and open it up to meaning. From this point of view the vocation of philosophy is a 'vocation devoted to the open'. This vocation marks a combat between the world of philosophy and the world of technique since the latter is the accomplishment of closed nihilism.

The analytic orientation holds the aim of philosophy to be the strict demarcation of those utterances which have meaning and those which do not. The aim is to demarcate what can be said and what it is impossible or illegitimate to say. The essential instrument of analytic philosophy is the logical and grammatical analysis of utterances, and ultimately of the entire language. This time the central concept is not interpretation but *the rule*. The task of philosophy is to discover those rules that ensure an agreement about meaning. The fundamental opposition here is between what can be regulated and what cannot be regulated, or what conforms to a recognized law assuring an agreement about meaning, and what eludes all explicit laws, thus falling into illusion or discordance. For the analytic orientation, the aim of philosophy is therapeutic and critical. It is a question of curing us of the illusions and the aberrations of language that divide us, by isolating what has no meaning, and by returning to rules which are transparent to all.

Finally, the postmodern orientation holds the aim of philosophy to be the deconstruction of the accepted facts of our modernity. In particular, postmodern philosophy proposes to dissolve the great constructions of the nineteenth century to which we remain captive – the idea of the historical subject, the idea of progress, the idea of revolution, the idea of humanity and the ideal of science. Its aim is to show that these great constructions are outdated, that we live in the multiple, that there are no great epics of history or of thought; that there is an irreducible plurality of registers and languages in thought as in action; registers so diverse and heterogeneous that no great idea can totalize or reconcile them. At base, the objective of postmodern philosophy is to deconstruct the idea of totality – to the extent that philosophy itself finds itself destabilized. Consequently, the postmodern orientation activates what might be called mixed practices, de-totalized practices, or impure thinking practices. It situates thought on the outskirts, in areas that cannot be circumscribed. In particular, it installs philosophical thought at the periphery of art, and proposes an untotalizable mixture of the conceptual method of philosophy and the sense-orientated enterprise of art.

The common themes of the three orientations of philosophy

Do these three orientations – so summarily described – have anything in common? Does anything allow us to say that, despite this diversity, features can be found which signal a unity of contemporary philosophy? I would suggest that there are two principal features that the three orientations, hermeneutic, analytic and postmodern, have in common. It is these common features which signal that the three orientations of philosophy are all *contemporary*, and that however different they may be, their destiny is joined: they do not simply provide one possible division of thought but rather provide three expressions of the same demands that our epoch makes on philosophy.

The first of these features is negative. All three orientations hold that we are at the end of metaphysics, that philosophy is no longer in a position to sustain its *locus classicus*; that is, the great figure of the metaphysical proposition. In a certain sense, these three orientations maintain that philosophy is itself situated within the end of philosophy, or that philosophy is announcing a certain end of itself.

We can immediately give three examples. It is clear that for Heidegger the theme of the end is the central element of his thinking. For Heidegger our time is characterized by the closure of the history of metaphysics, and thus of an entire epoch going back to Plato, an entire epoch of the history of being and thought. This closure is first realized in the distress and dereliction of the injunction of technology.

No philosophy could be further from Heidegger's than Carnap's. Yet Carnap also announces the end of any possibility of metaphysics because, for him, metaphysics consists of nothing more than utterances that are non-regulated and devoid of meaning. The aim of analytic therapy is to cure the metaphysical symptom; that is, to cure the patient of utterances whose analysis shows that they cannot give rise to assent because they are devoid of meaning.

If we take Jean-François Lyotard, one of his central themes is what he calls 'the end of the great narratives' – the great narratives of the revolution, of the proletariat, and of progress. Once more we have an 'end'; the end of the great narratives being the end of the great configurations of the subject and history that have been associated with modern metaphysics.

We find then a theme common to the three orientations, which is the theme of an end, of a drawing to a close, of an accomplishment. This theme can be articulated in another way: the ideal of truth as it was put forth by classical philosophy has come to its end. For the idea of truth we must substitute the idea of the plurality of meanings. This opposition between the classical ideal of truth and the modern theme of the polyvalence of meaning is, in my opinion, an essential opposition. We might say in a schematic, but not inexact way, that contemporary philosophy institutes the passage from a truth-orientated philosophy to a meaning-orientated philosophy.

In each of these three principal orientations, contemporary philosophy puts the category of truth on trial, and with it the classical figure of philosophy. That is what these three orientations have in common on the negative side. What they have in common on the positive side – and this is crucial – is the central place accorded to the question of language. The philosophy of this century has become principally a meditation on language, on its capacities, its rules, and on what it authorizes as far as thought is concerned. This is clear in the very definition of the orientations I have been talking about: the hermeneutic orientation, in a certain sense, always consists of the interpretation of speech acts; the analytic orientation consists of the confrontation between utterances and the rules which govern them; and the postmodern orientation promotes the idea of a multiplicity of sentences, fragments, and forms of discourse in the absence of homogeneity. Language has thus become the great historical transcendental of our times.

To recapitulate, contemporary philosophy has two fundamental axioms, common to all three orientations. The first is that the metaphysics of truth has become impossible. This axiom is negative.

Philosophy can no longer pretend to be what it had for a long time decided to be, that is, a search for truth. The second axiom is that language is the crucial site of thought because that is where the question of meaning is at stake. Consequently, the question of meaning replaces the classical question of truth.

The flaws in contemporary philosophy

My conviction is that these two axioms represent a real danger for thinking in general and for philosophy in particular. I think that their development and their infinitely subtle, complex and brilliant formulation, as found in contemporary philosophy, render philosophy incapable of sustaining the desire which is proper to it in the face of the pressure exerted by the contemporary world. These axioms cannot give philosophy the means to sustain its desire under the quadruple form of revolt, logic, universality and risk.

If philosophy is essentially a meditation on language, it will not succeed in removing the obstacle that the specialization and fragmentation of the world opposes to universality. To accept the universe of language as the absolute horizon of philosophical thought in fact amounts to accepting the fragmentation and the illusion of communication – for the truth of our world is that there are as many languages as there are communities, activities or kinds of knowledge. I agree that there *is* a multiplicity of language games. This, however, forces philosophy – if it wants to preserve the desire for universality – to establish itself elsewhere than within this multiplicity, so as not to be exclusively subordinated to it. If not, philosophy will become what in one way it mostly is, an infinite description of the multiplicity of language games.

Or else, but this would be even worse, philosophy might elect one particular language, claiming that the latter is the only one that can save it. We know what this leads to. Heidegger explicitly upheld the thesis of the intrinsic philosophical value, first of the Greek language, and then of the German language. He said: 'Being speaks Greek.' He said that the German language was, in a way, the only language in which thought could sustain the challenge of its destiny. And there is an ineluctable connection between this election of a language and the political position that resulted in Heidegger's commitment to German nationalism in the criminal form given to it by Nazism.

As for analytic philosophy, it is absolutely clear that it accords a unilateral privilege to scientific language as the language in which rules are both explicit and the most adequate to the subject of the language. This is clear in the way in which sense and non-sense are differentiated by presenting the distinction in the guise of a rule, as can be seen in mathematics and scientific language in general. But this privilege is itself philosophically dangerous because it leads directly to a contempt for all sites and spaces which rebel against the configuration of scientific language. And the privilege accorded this language isolates a figure of rationality that is ineluctably accompanied by disdain or contempt or the closing of one's eyes to the fact that even today the overwhelming majority of humanity is out of reach of such a language.

On the other hand, if the category of truth is ignored, if we never confront anything but the polyvalence of meaning, then philosophy will never assume the challenge that is put out to it by a world subordinated to the merchandising of money and information. This world is an anarchy of more or less regulated, more or less coded fluxes, wherein money, products and images are exchanged. If philosophy is to sustain its desire in such a world, it must propose a principle of interruption. It must be able to propose to thought something that can interrupt this endless regime of circulation. Philosophy must examine the possibility of a point of interruption – not because all this must be interrupted – but because thought at least must be able to extract itself from this circulation and take possession of itself once again as something other than an object of circulation. It is obvious that such a point of interruption can only be an unconditional requirement; that is, something which is submitted to thought with no other condition than itself and which is neither exchangeable nor capable of being put into circulation. That there be such a point of interruption, that there be at least one unconditional requirement, is, in my opinion, a condition *sine qua non* for the existence of philosophy. In the absence of such a point, *all there is* is the general circulation of knowledge, information, merchandise, money and images. In my opinion, this unconditional requirement cannot be solely supported by the proposition of the polyvalence of meaning. It also needs the reconstruction or re-emergence of the category of truth.

We are subjected to the media's inconsistency of images and commentaries. What can be opposed to this? I do not think that anything can be opposed to it except the patient search for at least one truth, and perhaps several; without which the essential illogicism of mass communication will impose its temporal carnival.

Philosophy also requires that we throw the dice against the obsession for security, that we interrupt the calculus of life determined by security. But what chance has philosophy of winning, except in the name of a value that would ordain this risk and give it a minimum of consistency and weight? Here again I believe it is vain to imagine that in the absence of a principle of truth, one can oppose an existential gamble to the calculus of life, a gamble that could give rise to something that could be called liberty.

Given the axioms of contemporary philosophy, can the desire for philosophy be maintained in the world such as it is? Can we maintain the four dimensions of revolt, logic, universality and risk against the four contemporary obstacles: merchandise, communication, technical division and the obsession with security?

I submit that this cannot be done within the framework of the hermeneutic, analytic or postmodern orientations of philosophy. In my opinion these orientations are too strongly committed to the polyvalence of meaning and the plurality of languages. There is something in them that goes too far in reflecting the physiognomy of the world itself. They are too compatible with our world to be able to sustain the rupture or distance that philosophy requires.

Towards a new style of philosophy

My position is to break with these frameworks of thought, to find another philosophical style, a style other than that of interpretation, of logical grammarian analysis, or of polyvalence and language games – that is, to rediscover a foundational style, a decided style, a style in the school of a Descartes for example.

Such a position can be supported by two ideas, both simple, but in my opinion both preliminary to the development of philosophy. The first idea is that language is not the absolute horizon of thought. The great linguistic turn of philosophy, or the absorption of philosophy into the meditation on language, must be reversed. In the *Cratylus*, which is concerned with language from beginning to end, Plato says, 'We philosophers do not take as our point of departure words, but things.' Whatever may be the difficulty or obscurity of this statement, I am for philosophy's revivifying the idea that it does not take as its point of departure words, but things. Needless to say, it must be acknowledged that a language always constitutes what can be called the historical matter of truth and of philosophy. A language always gives what I would call the colour of philosophy, its tonality, and its inflexion. All these singular figures are proposed to us by language. But I would also maintain that this is not the essential principle of the organization of thought. The principle that philosophy cannot renounce is that of its universal transmissibility, whatever the prescription of style or colour, whatever its connection to such or such a language. Philosophy cannot renounce that its address is directed to everyone, in principle if not in fact, and that it does not exclude from this address linguistic, national, religious or racial communities. Philosophy privileges no language, not even the one it is written in. Philosophy is not enclosed within the pure formal ideal of scientific language. Its natural element is language, but, within that natural element, it institutes a universal address.

The second idea is that the singular and irreducible role of philosophy is to establish a fixed point within discourse, a point of interruption, a point of discontinuity, an unconditional point. Our world is marked by its speed: the speed of historical change; the speed of technical change; the speed of communications; of transmissions; and even the speed with which human beings establish connections with one another. This speed exposes us to the danger of a very great incoherency. It is because things, images and relations circulate so quickly that we do not even have the time to measure the extent of this incoherency. Speed is the mask of inconsistency. Philosophy must propose a retardation process. It must construct a time for thought, which, in the face of the injunction to speed, will constitute a time of its own. I consider this a singularity of philosophy; that its thinking is leisurely, because today revolt requires leisureliness and not speed. This thinking, slow and consequently rebellious, is alone capable of establishing the fixed point, whatever it may be, whatever its name may be, which we need in order to sustain the desire of philosophy.

At base, it is a question of philosophically reconstructing, with a slowness which will insulate us from the speed of the world, the category of truth – not as it is passed down to us by metaphysics, but rather as we are able to reconstitute it, taking into consideration the world as it is. It is a question of reorganizing philosophy around this reconstruction and giving it the time and space that are proper to it. This supposes that philosophy will no longer be in pursuit of the world, that it will stop trying to be as rapid as the world, because by wanting to be as rapid, philosophy dissolves itself at the very heart of its desire, no longer being in a state to maintain its revolt, to reconstitute its logic, to know what a universal address is, or to take a chance and liberate existence.

The world questions philosophy

Evidently the problem is one of knowing if, in the world as it is, there is the slightest chance for such an enterprise to flourish or be heard, or if what is proposed here is yet another vain invocation. There is no doubt that philosophy is ill. As always, the problem is knowing whether this illness is mortal or not, knowing what the diagnostic is, and knowing whether the proposed remedy is not in fact, as is often the case, exactly what will finish off the patient. Truth is suffering from two illnesses. In my opinion, it is suffering from linguistic relativism, that is, its entanglement in the problematic of the disparity of meanings; and it is also suffering from historical pessimism, including about itself.

My hypothesis is that although philosophy is ill, it is less ill than it thinks it is, less ill than it says it is. One of the characteristics of contemporary philosophy is to elaborate page after page on its own mortal illnesses. But you know, when it is the patient who says he is ill, there is always a chance that it is at least in part an imaginary illness. And I think that this is the case, because the world itself, despite all the negative pressures it exerts on the desire of philosophy, the world, that is the people who live in it and think in it, this world, is asking something of philosophy. Yet philosophy is too morose to respond due to the morbidity of its own vision of itself.

Four reasons make me believe that the world is asking something of philosophy.

The first reason is that we now know that there is no chance that the human sciences will replace philosophy. The awareness of this seems to me to be fairly widespread since the human sciences have become the home of the statistical sciences. The human sciences are thereby themselves caught up in the circulation of meaning and its polyvalence, because they measure rates of circulation. That is their purpose. At base they are in the service of polls, election predictions, demographic averages, epidemiological rates, tastes and distastes, and all that certainly makes for interesting labour. But this statistical and numerical information has nothing to do with what humanity, nor what each absolutely singular being, is about. Everyone knows that the singular is always, in the final analysis, the true centre of any decision which counts, and that all truth is first presented in the form of the absolutely singular – as can be seen in scientific invention, artistic creation, political innovation or the encounter that comprises love. In every place where, in some way, a truth is pronounced on existence, it is founded on a singularity. Averages, statistics, sociology, history, demography, or polls are not capable of teaching us what the history of a truth is. Philosophy is thus required by the world to be a philosophy of singularity, to be capable of pronouncing and thinking the singular, which is precisely what the general apparatus of human sciences does not have as its vocation. That is the first reason.

The second reason is that we are witnessing the ruin of the great collective enterprises that we once imagined carried within themselves the seeds of emancipation and truth. We know now that there are no such great emancipatory forces, that there is neither progress, nor proletariat, nor any such thing. We know that we are not caught up by such forces and that there is no hope for us of sustaining our desire by simply incorporating ourselves into such a force, or by being a member of such a force. What does this mean? This means that each of us, and not only the philosopher, knows that today, if we are confronted with the inhuman, we must make our own decision and speak in our own name. One cannot hide behind any great collective configuration, any supposed force, any metaphysical totality which might take a position in one's stead. But in order to take a position in one's own name when faced with the inhuman, a fixed point is needed for the decision. An unconditional principle is needed to regulate both the decision and the assent. This is what everyone calls today the necessity of a return to ethics. But let us not be mistaken. Philosophically, the return to ethics necessitates the return of an unconditional principle. There is a moment when one must be able to say that this is right and that is wrong, in light of the evidence of the principle. There cannot be an infinite regression of quibbling and calculating. There must also be utterances of which it can be said they are unconditionally true. We know very well that when a position on a given question and an agreement on that position are demanded, as a last resort it is necessary to find a position which will be unconditionally true for everyone. Thus one cannot say that each of us must take a position in his or her own name once faced with the inhuman, without re-engaging philosophy in the dimension of truth. And this is required by the world as it is, and this is required of philosophy.

The third reason is connected to the recent rise of reactive or archaic passions; that is, the rise of cultural, religious, national and racist passions.

These historically observable phenomena have also given birth to a demand upon philosophy. Confronted by these passions once again, philosophy is urged to speak about where reason lies, for these passions are the contemporary figures of irrational archaism and they carry with them death and devastation. Philosophy is required to make a pronouncement about contemporary rationality. We know that this rationality cannot be the repetition of classical rationalism, but we also know that we cannot do without it, if we do not want to find ourselves in a position of extreme intellectual weakness when faced with the threat of these reactive passions. We must then forge a rational philosophy in this sense of the term; that is, in the sense that philosophy must reiterate, under the conditions of the times, what it has already resolved.

The fourth and final reason is that the world we live in is a vulnerable, precarious world. It is in no way a world stabilized within the unity of its history. We must not allow the global acceptance of the themes of liberal economy and representative democracy to dissimulate the fact that the world the twentieth century has given birth to is a violent and fragile world. Its material, ideological and intellectual foundations are disparate, disunited and largely inconsistent. This world does not announce the serenity of a linear development, but rather a series of dramatic crises and paradoxical events. Take two recent examples, the Gulf War and the fall of bureaucratic socialism. Add to these the war in Bosnia and the Rwandan massacres. But do not be mistaken; these events are only the first in a long series. Philosophy is required to ensure that thought can receive and accept the drama of the event without anxiety. We do not fundamentally need a philosophy of the structure of things. We need a philosophy open to the irreducible singularity of what happens, a philosophy that can be fed and nourished by the surprise of the unexpected. Such a philosophy would then be a philosophy of the event. This too is required of philosophy by the world, by the world as it is.

A new doctrine of the subject

What is thus demanded of us by the world is a philosophy of singularity, a philosophy of contemporary rationality, and a philosophy of the event. This is a programme in itself. To accomplish this programme we must go beyond the three principal tendencies of philosophy I have described. We need a more determined and more imperative philosophy, but one that is, at the same time, more modest, more remote from the world and more descriptive. A philosophy which is a rational intertwining of the singularity of the event and of truth. A philosophy open to chance, but a chance submitted to the law of reason; a philosophy maintaining unconditional principles, unconditional but submitted to a non-theological law.

This will allow us to propose a new doctrine of the subject – and I think this is the essential objective. We will be able to say what a subject is in terms other than those of Descartes, Kant or Hegel. This subject will be singular and not universal, and it will be singular because it will always be an event that constitutes the subject as a truth.

In view of this programme, it can be said, it's true, that the metaphysics of truth is ruined and classical rationalism is insufficient. But in a way the deconstruction of metaphysics and the contestation of rationalism are also insufficient. The world needs philosophy to be re-founded upon the ruins of metaphysics as combined and blended with the modern criticism of metaphysics.

I am convinced, and this is the reason for my optimism, that the world needs philosophy more than philosophy thinks. Philosophy is ill, it might be dying, but I am sure that the world (the world, neither a God nor a prophet, but the world) is saying to philosophy: 'Get up and walk!'

Note

1   Translator's note: This paper was given in Sydney in 1999. Its original title was 'The desire of philosophy and the contemporary world'. In French, the phrase 'le désir de philosophie' is ambiguous as to the syntactic status of 'philosophie'. In the objective sense of the genitive, it is philosophy which is desired. However, in the subjective sense, it can also be said that it is philosophy which desires, or that there is a desire which traverses philosophy.

2
Philosophy and truth

It is time to advance four fundamental theses on truth:[1]

1   Regarding the question of truth, the Heideggerean edifice leaves no other solution than that of the poem.
2   In order to destroy this edifice and find another solution, we cannot reverse the historical process delineated by Heidegger himself. On the contrary, we must assume, against the analytic tradition, that the essence of truth remains inaccessible if its question is enclosed in the narrow form of the judgement or the proposition. Yet, at the same time, we cannot allow Heidegger his melancholic vision of the loss of the un-veiling.
3   We must conceive of a truth both as the construction of a fidelity to an event, and as the generic potency of a transformation of a domain of knowledge.
4   All the categories by which the essence of a truth can be submitted to thought are negative: undecidability, indiscernibility, the generic not-all (*pas-tout*), and the unnameable. The ethic of truths resides entirely in the measure taken of this negative, or in other words, in the limitations placed on the potency of truth by the hazards of its construction.

We shall select three references from the Heideggerean doctrine of truth. The first:

In becoming a property of the proposition, not only does truth displace its locus; it transforms its essence.

This must be understood as stating that the entire effect of the decline of thought, which is also the decline of being, is manifested in the fact that truth is presented, after Plato, as localizable in the proposition. This localization is also a de-naturing. Nothing of the truth, in its authentic sense, remains accessible if we allow that the phenomenon of truth occurs in the proposition.

The context of the second passage is Heidegger's question concerning what the major points of meditation must be if one wishes to capture the distress of Europe in thought. For Heidegger, the essential events of this distress are the flight of the gods, the destruction of the earth, the becoming social of man and the preponderance of the mediocre. In this passage, Heidegger tells us that for such a meditation one thing is decisive:

> The mutation occurs through the interpretation of spirit as intellect, the latter being understood as the simple faculty to reason correctly in theoretical and practical considerations, and as the estimation of things already presented.

It is clear that spirit can only be interpreted as intellect if it manipulates truth in the form of a proposition. For a proposition is effectively the linguistic phenomenon of any estimation of things, insofar as they are things already presented. Consequently, the de-naturing of the essence of truth, which localizes it in the proposition, is the condition of possibility at the origins of Western distress.

The third passage concerns what can be said about an access to truth freed from the form of the proposition. What is a language that expresses the truth otherwise than in the scientific or logical form of the proposition? A language that is related, not to things already presented, but to things which have not yet arrived? There is no doubt about the answer; such a language can be found in the poem. Heidegger writes:

> In poetry which is authentic and great, an essential superiority of the spirit reigns over everything which is purely science. A superiority in virtue of which the poet always speaks as if being was expressed and called upon for the first time.

Thus, for Heidegger, if the declining destiny of being is to de-nature truth in the proposition – if the proposition, commanding the interpretation of the spirit as pragmatic intellect, governs the ravage of the earth – then the only real recourse lies in the poem. In turn, the poem is explicitly opposed to the mathematical because, for Heidegger, the mathematical is nothing other than the transparent triumph of the propositional form of truth. When the proposition reigns, when the intellect reigns, then he says, 'the Being of beings becomes thinkable within the pure thought of the mathematical'.

My entire argument will be to acknowledge that truth remains unthinkable if we attempt to contain it within the form of the proposition. But that furthermore, conceiving truth as a historical process requires neither the thesis of the Platonic decline, nor the attribution of a superiority of essence for poetry over the mathematical, or over any other type of truth procedure.

Our epoch is most certainly that of a rupture with all that Philippe Lacoue-Labarthe has shown to depend on the motif of *mimesis*. One of the forms of this motif, which explicitly attaches truth to imitation, is the conception of truth as a relation: a relation of appropriateness between the intellect and the thing intellected; a relation of adequation, which always supposes, as Heidegger very well perceived, that truth be localizable in the form of a proposition.

Modern philosophy is a criticism of truth as adequation. Truth is not *adequation rei et intellectus*. Truth is not limited to the form of judgement. Hegel shows that truth is a path. Heidegger suggests that it is a historical destiny.

I will start from the following idea: a truth is, first of all, something new. What transmits, what repeats, we shall call *knowledge*. Distinguishing truth from knowledge is essential. It is a distinction that is already made in the work of Kant: the distinction between *reason* and *understanding*. It is a capital distinction for Heidegger: the distinction between truth – *aletheia* – and cognition or science – *techne*.

If a truth is something new, what is the essential philosophical problem concerning truth? It is the problem of its appearance and its 'becoming'. A truth must be submitted to thought, not as a judgement, but as a process in the real.

The schema you have represents the 'becoming' of a truth.

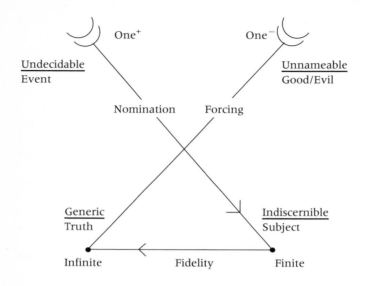

For the process of a truth to begin, something must happen. What there already is – the situation of knowledge as such – generates nothing other than repetition. For a truth to affirm its newness, there must be a *supplement*. This supplement is committed to chance. It is unpredictable, incalculable. It is beyond what is. I call it an event. A truth thus appears, in its newness, because an evental supplement interrupts repetition.

Examples: the appearance, with Aeschylus, of theatrical Tragedy; the irruption, with Galileo, of mathematical physics; an amorous encounter which changes a whole life; the French Revolution of 1792.

An event is linked to the notion of the *undecidable*. Take the statement: 'This event belongs to the situation.' If it is possible to decide, using the rules of established knowledge, whether this statement is true or false, then the so-called event is not an event. Its occurrence would be calculable within the situation. Nothing would permit us to say: here begins a truth. On the basis of the undecidability of an event's belonging to a situation a *wager* has to be made. This is why a truth begins with an *axiom of truth*. It begins with a groundless decision – the decision to *say* that the event has taken place.

The undecidability of the event induces the appearance of a *subject* of the event. Such a subject is constituted by an utterance in the form of a wager. This utterance is as follows: 'This event has taken place, it is something which I can neither evaluate, nor demonstrate, but to which I shall be faithful.' To begin with, a subject is what fixes an undecidable event, because he or she takes the chance of deciding upon it.

This decision opens up the infinite procedure of verification of the true. This procedure is the examination, within the situation, of the consequences of the axiom that decided upon the event. Such a procedure is an exercise of fidelity. Nothing regulates its course, since the axiom that supports it has arbitrated outside of any rule of established knowledge. The procedure thus follows a chance-driven course, a course without a concept.

But what is a pure choice, a choice without a concept? Obviously, it is a choice confronted by two *indiscernible* terms. Two terms are indiscernible if no effect of language allows them to be distinguished. But if no formula of language discerns two terms in a situation, then it is certain that the choice of verifying one term rather than the other will find no support in the objectivity of their difference. Such a choice is then an absolutely pure choice, free from any other presupposition than that of having to choose, and with no indication marking the proposed terms, the term which will allow the verification of the consequences of the axiom to commence.

This means that the subject of a truth demands the indiscernible. The indiscernible organizes the pure point of the Subject in the process of verification. A subject is what disappears between two indiscernibles. A subject is a throw of the dice which does not abolish chance, but which accomplishes chance through the verification of the axiom that founds it as a subject. What was decided concerning the undecidable event must pass by *this* term, indiscernible from its other. Such is the local act of a truth; it consists in a pure choice between two indiscernibles. Such an act is thus absolutely finite.

For example, the work of Sophocles is a subject for the artistic truth – or procedure – of Greek tragedy, a truth begun by the event of Aeschylus. This work is *creation*; that is, a pure choice in what, before it, was indiscernible. And it is a finite work. However, Tragedy itself, as an artistic truth, continues to infinity. The work of Sophocles is a finite subject of this infinite truth. In the same way, the scientific truth decided by Galileo is pursued to infinity. But the laws of physics which have been successively invented are finite subjects of this truth.

The trajectory of a truth begins with an undecidable event. It finds its act in a finite subject confronted by the indiscernible. The course of verification of the true continues; it invests the situation with successive choices. Little by little the contour of a subset of the situation is outlined, in which the effects of the evental axiom are verified. It is clear that this subset is infinite, that it remains interminable. Yet it is possible to state that, if we suppose its termination, then such a subset will ineluctably be one that no predicate can unify – an untotalizable subset, a subset that can be neither constructed nor named in the language. Such subsets are called *generic* subsets. We shall say that a truth, supposed as finished, is generic.

In contrast, if a succession of pure choices engendered a subset which could be unified under a predication, then the course of the truth would have to have been secretly governed by a law, or the indiscernibles wherein the subject finds its act would have to have been, in reality, discerned by some superior understanding. But no such law exists. Invention and creation remain incalculable. So the path of a truth cannot coincide in infinity with any concept. Consequently, the verified terms compose, or rather will have composed, if we suppose their infinite totalization, a generic subset of the Universe. Indiscernible in its act, or as Subject, a truth is generic in its result, or in its being. It is withdrawn from any unification by a single predicate.

For example, after Galileo, there does not exist a closed and unified subset of knowledge that we could call 'physics'. What does exist is an infinite and open set of laws and experiments; and even if we suppose the completion of this set, there is no way it could be captured by a single formula of language. There is no law of physical laws. As such, 'the physical' is a generic set, both infinite and indistinct – this is what the *being* of physical truth is. In the same way, after the 1792 Revolution, there were all sorts of revolutionary politics. But there is no single political formula which totalizes these revolutionary politics. The set called 'revolutionary politics' is a *generic* truth of the political.

What happens is that we can always *anticipate* the idea of a completed generic truth. The generic being of a truth is never presented. A truth is uncompletable. But what we can know, on a formal level, is that a truth will always have taken place as a generic infinity. This allows the possible fictioning of the effects of such a truth having-taken-place. That is, the subject can make the hypothesis of a Universe where this truth, of which the subject is a local point, will have completed its generic totalization. I call the anticipatory hypothesis of the generic being of a truth, a *forcing*. A forcing is the powerful fiction of a *completed* truth. Starting with such a fiction, I can *force* new bits of knowledge, without even *verifying* this knowledge.

Thus, Galileo was able to make the hypothesis that all nature can be written in mathematical language, which is the hypothesis of a *complete* physics. On the basis of this anticipation, he *forces* his Aristotelian adversary to abandon his position. In the same way, someone in love can say, 'I will always love you,' which is the anticipating hypothesis of a truth of integral love. On the basis of this hypothesis, they force the other to come to know and treat them differently.

The *construction* of a truth is made by a choice within the indiscernible. It is made locally, within the finite. But the *potency* of a truth depends on the hypothetical forcing. It consists in saying: '*If* we suppose the generic infinity of a truth to be completed, *then* such or such a bit of knowledge must imperatively be transformed.'

The problem is to know whether such a potency of anticipation is *total*. If we can *force* all the bits of knowledge concerned then we end up with the romantic problem of absolute love, the scientific problem of science as integral truth, and the political problem of totalitarianism. This problem can be expressed simply: can we, from the basis of a finite Subject of a truth, *name* and *force into knowledge* all the elements that this truth concerns? How far does the anticipating potency of generic infinity go? My answer is that there is *always*, in any situation, a real point that *resists* this potency.

I call this point the *unnameable* of the situation. It is what, within the situation, never has a name in the eyes of truth. A term that consequently remains *unforceable*. This term fixes the limit of the potency of a truth. The unnameable is what is excluded from having a proper name, and what is alone in such exclusion. The unnameable is then the proper of the proper, so singular in its singularity that it does not even tolerate having a proper name. The unnameable is the point where the situation in its most intimate being is submitted to thought; in the pure presence that no knowledge can circumscribe. The unnameable is something like the inexpressible *real* of everything a truth authorizes to be said.

For example, the mathematical consists of pure deduction. We always suppose that it contains no contradictions. But Gödel showed that it is impossible to demonstrate, *within* a mathematical theory, that this very theory is non-contradictory. A mathematical truth thus cannot *force* the non-contradictoriness of mathematics. We will say that non-contradiction is the *unnameable* of the mathematical. And it is clear that this unnameable is the *real* of the mathematical; for if a mathematical theory is contradictory, it is destroyed.

Consequently, a reasonable ethic of mathematics is to not wish to force this point; to accept that a mathematical truth is never *complete*. But this reasonable ethic is difficult to maintain. As can be seen with scientism, or with totalitarianism, there is always a desire for the omnipotence of the True. There lies the root of Evil. Evil is the will to name *at any price*.

Usually it is said that Evil is lies, ignorance, or deadly stupidity. The condition of Evil is much rather the process of a truth. There is Evil only insofar as there is an axiom of truth at the point of the undecidable, a path of truth at the point of the indiscernible, an anticipation of being for the generic, and the forcing of a nomination at the point of the unnameable.

If the forcing of the unnameable exclusion is a disaster, this is because it affects the entire situation, by pursuing singularity itself, whose emblem is the unnameable. In this sense, the desire in fictioning to suppress the unnameable frees the destructive capacity contained in all truth.

As such the ethic of a truth resides entirely in a sort of caution as far as its powers are concerned. The effect of the undecidable, of the indiscernible and of the generic, or in other words, the effect of the event, the subject and the truth, must recognize the unnameable as a *limitation* of its path.

Finally, Evil is the desire for 'Everything-to-be-said.' To contain Evil, the potency of the True must be *measured*.

What helps us is the rigorous study of the *negative* characters of the path of truth: the event is undecidable; the subject is linked to the indiscernible; truth itself is generic, untotalizable; and the halting point of its potency is the unnameable. This gives us four negative categories. The philosophical study of these categories is capital. It can be fuelled by each and every thought event that shapes our times.

The undecidability of an event and the suspension of its name, are both features of politics that are particularly active today. It is clear for a French man or woman that the events of May '68 continue to comprise an unattested or anonymous promise. But even the 1792 revolution or the Bolshevik revolution of 1917 remain partly undecided as to what they prescribe for philosophy.

The theory of indiscernibles is in itself an entire mathematical theory, from the Galois groups to the indiscernibles in the theory of models. But we can also say that one of the aims of contemporary poetics is to found in language a point of indiscernibility between prose and poetry, or between image and thought.

The theory of the generic is at the heart of the ultimate forms of the logic of sets, following upon Paul Cohen's theorem. But the modern politics of emancipation, delivered from the dialectical scheme of classes and parties, has as its aim a 'generic' democracy, a promotion of the commonplace, of equality abstracted from any predicate. And a whole field of prose, such as Samuel Beckett's, tries, by successive subtractions, to designate the naked existence of a generic humanity.

Finally, the unnameable is the central motif of the thought of the political that wishes to submit Nazism to thought; as it is of the poet who explores the limits of the force of language; as it is for the mathematician who looks for the undefinables of a structure; as it is for the person in love tormented by what love bears of the sexual unnameable.

Thus the ethic of truths, relation or un-relation, between the construction of a truth and its potency, is that by which we take the measure of what our times are capable of, as well as what our times are worth. Such is, in a word, the very task of philosophy.

Note

1 This paper was given in Sydney in 1999. Its original title was 'The ethic of truths: construction and potency'.

3
Philosophy and politics

From Plato until the present day, there is one word which crystallizes the philosopher's concern in regard to politics: 'justice'.[1] The question that the philosopher addresses to politics can be formulated as: Can there be a just politics? Or a politics which *does justice* to thought?

Our point of departure must be the following: injustice is clear, justice is obscure. Those who have undergone injustice provide irrefutable testimony concerning the former. But who can testify for justice? Injustice has its affect: suffering, revolt. Nothing, however, signals justice: it presents itself neither as spectacle nor as sentiment.

Is our sole issue then that of saying that justice is merely the absence of injustice? Is justice nothing more than the empty neutrality of a double negation? I do not think so. Nor do I think that injustice is to be found on the side of the perceptible, or experience, or the subjective, while justice is found on the side of the intelligible, or reason, or the objective. Injustice is not the immediate disorder of that for which justice would provide an ideal order.

'Justice' is a word from philosophy; at least if we leave aside, as we must, its legal signification, which is entirely devoted to the police and the judiciary. Yet this word of philosophy is under condition. It is under the condition of the political. For philosophy knows that for the truths to which it testifies, it is incapable of rendering them real in the world. Even Plato knows that while the philosopher would probably have to be king for there to be justice, the very possibility of such royalty's existence would not depend upon philosophy. It would depend upon political circumstances; the latter remain irreducible.

We will term 'justice' the name by which a philosophy designates the possible truth of a political orientation.

The vast majority of empirical political orientations have nothing to do with truth. We know this. They organize a repulsive mixture of power and opinions. The subjectivity that animates them is that of the tribe and the lobby, of electoral nihilism and the blind confrontation of communities. Philosophy has nothing to say about such politics; for philosophy thinks thought alone, whereas these orientations present themselves explicitly as unthinking, or as non-thought. The only subjective element which is important to such orientations is that of *interest*.

Historically speaking, there have been some political orientations that have had or will have a connection with a truth, a truth of the collective as such. They are rare attempts, and they are often brief, but they alone can act as a condition of philosophy's thinking.

These political sequences are *singularities*: they do not trace a destiny, nor do they construct a monumental history. Philosophy, however, can distinguish a common feature among them. This feature is that from the people they engage these orientations require nothing but their strict generic humanity. In their principles of action, these orientations take no account of the particularity of interests. They induce a representation of the capacity of the collective which refers its agents to the strictest equality.

What does 'equality' signify here? Equality means that a political actor is represented under the sole sign of his or her specifically human capacity. Interest is not a specifically human capacity. All living beings protect their interests as an imperative for survival. The capacity which is specifically human is that of thought, and thought is nothing other than that by which the path of a truth seizes and traverses the human animal.

Therefore, for a political orientation to be worthy of submission to philosophy under the idea 'justice', its unique general axiom must be: people think, people are capable of truth. When Saint-Just defined *public consciousness* before the Convention in April 1794, he was thinking of a strictly egalitarian recognition of the capacity for truth: 'May you have a public consciousness, for all hearts are equal as to sentiments of good and bad, and this consciousness is made up of the tendency of the people towards the general good.' During an entirely different political sequence in the Cultural Revolution in China, the same principle can be found: for example, in the sixteen-point decision of 8 August 1966, 'Let the masses educate themselves in this great revolutionary movement, let them

53

determine themselves the distinction between what is just and what is not.'

Thus a political orientation touches upon truth provided that it is founded upon the egalitarian principle of a capacity to discern the just or the good: philosophy understands both terms under the sign of a collective's capacity for truth.

It is very important to note that 'equality' does not refer to anything objective. It is not a question of an equality of status, of income, of function, and even less of the supposedly egalitarian dynamics of contracts or reforms. Equality is subjective. It is equality with respect to public consciousness for Saint-Just, or with respect to political mass movement for Mao Tse-tung. Such equality is in no way a social programme. Moreover, it has nothing to do with the social. It is a political maxim, a prescription. Political equality is not what we want or plan, it is what we declare under fire of the event, here and now, as what is, and not as what should be. In the same way, for philosophy, 'justice' cannot be a State programme: 'justice' is the qualification of an egalitarian political orientation in act.

The difficulty with most doctrines of justice is that they seek a definition of justice and then they try to find means for its realization. But justice, which is the philosophical name for the egalitarian political maxim, cannot be defined. For equality is not an objective for action, it is an axiom of action. There is no political orientation linked to truth which does not possess an affirmation – an affirmation which has neither a guarantee nor a proof – of a universal capacity for political truth. Here thought cannot use the scholastic method of definitions. It must use a method which proceeds via the comprehension of axioms.

'Justice' is nothing other than one of the words by which a philosophy attempts to *seize* the egalitarian axiom inherent in a veritable political sequence. This axiom is given in singular statements, characteristic of the sequence, such as Saint-Just's definition of public consciousness, or Mao's thesis on the immanent self-education of the revolutionary mass movement.

Justice is not a concept as such, entailing a search for its more or less approximate realizations in the empirical world. Rather, once justice is conceived of as an operator of capture for egalitarian political orientations – *true* political orientations – then it defines an effective, axiomatic, and immediate subjective figure. This is what gives all its depth to Samuel Beckett's surprising affirmation in *How It Is*: 'In any case we are within justice, I've never heard anyone say the contrary.' That is, justice – which captures the latent axiom of a political subject – necessarily designates not what must be, but what is. Either the egalitarian axiom is present in political statements, or it is not. Consequently, either we are within justice, or we are not. This also means: either the political exists, in the sense that philosophy encounters thought within it, or it does not. But if it does, and if we relate to it immanently, then we are within justice.

Any definitional and programmatic approach to justice turns it into a dimension of the action of the State. But the State has nothing to do with justice, for the State is not a subjective and axiomatic figure. The State as such is indifferent or hostile to the existence of any political orientation which touches truths. The modern State aims solely at fulfilling certain functions, or at crafting a consensus of opinion. Its sole subjective dimension is that of transforming economic necessity – that is, the objective logic of Capital – into resignation or resentment. This is why any programmatic or State definition of justice changes the latter into its contrary: justice becomes the harmonization of the interplay of interests. But justice, which is the theoretical name for an axiom of equality, necessarily refers to an entirely *disinterested* subjectivity.

In other words, any politics of emancipation, or any politics which imposes an egalitarian maxim, is a thought in act. Thought is the specific mode by which a human animal is traversed and overcome by a truth. In such a subjectivization one goes beyond the limits of interest, such that the political process itself becomes indifferent to interests. It thus follows, as demonstrated by all political sequences which concern philosophy, that the State is incapable of recognizing anything appropriate to it in such a process.

The State, in its being, is indifferent to justice. Conversely, any political orientation which is a thought in act entails, in proportion to its force and its tenacity, serious trouble for the State. This is why political truth always manifests itself in times of trial and trouble. It follows that justice, far from being a possible category of state or social order, is what names the principles at work in rupture and disorder. Even Aristotle, whose entire goal is a fiction of political stability, declares at the beginning of Book 5 of his *Politics*: ὅλως γάρ τὸ ἴσον ζητοῦντες στασιάζουσιν; which can be translated as, 'Generally, it is the pursuers of equality who rise in rebellion.' However, Aristotle's conception is still a state conception; his idea of equality is empirical, objective and definitional. The veritable philosophical statement would rather be: Political statements bearing truth rise up in the absence of any state or social order. The latent egalitarian maxim is heterogeneous to the State. It is thus always during trouble and disorder that the subjective imperative of equality is affirmed. What the philosopher names 'justice' seizes the subjective *order* of a maxim, found within the ineluctable disorder to which the State of interests is exposed by that very order.

Finally, what does making a philosophical statement on justice, here and now, amount to?

First it is a matter of knowing which singular political orientations to call upon; that is, which ones are worth our trying to seize the thought specific to them via the resources of the philosophic apparatus – one of whose pieces is the word 'justice'.

This is not an easy job in today's confused and chaotic world, when Capital seems to triumph on the basis of its own weaknesses, and when *what is* fuses miserably with *what can be*. Identifying those rare sequences through which a political truth is constructed, without being discouraged by the propaganda of capitalistic parliamentarian government, is itself a sustained exercise of thought. Still more difficult is attempting – within the very order of practising politics – to be faithful to some egalitarian axiom, and finding contemporary statements of such.

Second, it is a matter of philosophically seizing the political orientations in question, whether they be of the past or the present. The task is then double:

1 To examine their statements and prescriptions in order to uncover the egalitarian nucleus which bears a universal signification.
2 To transform the generic category of 'justice' by submitting it to the test of singular statements; that is, to the irreducible specificity of how such statements bear forth and inscribe the egalitarian axiom in action.

Finally, it is a matter of showing that, thus transformed, the category of justice designates the contemporary figure of a political subject; furthermore, showing that it is by means of such a figure that philosophy assures, via its own names, the inscription of what our time is capable of in eternity.

This political subject has had several names: 'Citizen', for example, not in the sense of an elector or a city councillor, but in the sense the French Revolution gives to the word; there is also 'professional revolutionary', and 'grass-roots activist'. Without doubt, we live in a time in which this name is in suspense, in a time when *this subject's name must be found*.

In other words, even if we have a history, with neither continuity nor concept, of what 'justice' has been able to designate, we still do not know clearly what it designates today. Of course we know in an abstract sense, because 'justice' always signifies the philosophical capture of a latent egalitarian axiom. But this abstraction is useless. The imperative of philosophy is to seize the event of truths, their newness, and their precarious trajectory. It is not the concept that philosophy turns towards eternity as the communal dimension of thought, it is rather the singular process of a truth. It is in relation to its *own* epoch that philosophy tries to work out whether the hypothesis of the Eternal Return can be supported without ridicule or scandal.

Is the current state of political orientations such that philosophy can employ the category of justice? Is there not a risk here of confusing chalk with cheese, of reproducing the vulgar pretension of governments to render justice? When we see so many 'philosophers' attempting to appropriate for themselves state schemes with as little thought in them as Europe, democracy in the capitalist-parliamentary sense, liberty in the sense of pure opinion, or shameful nationalisms, when we see philosophy thus prostrated before the idols of the day, then clearly some pessimism is understandable.

But after all, the conditions for the exercise of philosophy have always been rigorous. The words of philosophy are always misused and turned around when these conditions are not observed. There have been intense political sequences in the twentieth century. There are faithful followers of these sequences. Here or there, in as yet incomparable situations, some statements envelop, in an inflexible and non-subjugated manner, the egalitarian axiom.

The collapse of the socialist States has itself a positive dimension. Certainly, it was a pure and simple collapse; no political orientation worthy of the name played the smallest part in it. And ever since, this political vacuity has not ceased to engender monsters. Yet these terrorist States incarnated the ultimate fiction of a justice which had the solidity of a body, of a justice which took the form of a governmental programme. What the collapse did was attest to the absurdity of such a representation. It frees justice and equality from any fictive incorporation. It returned them to their being, both volatile and obstinate, of free rein, of thought acting from and in the direction of a collective seized by its truth. The collapse of the socialist States teaches us that the ways of egalitarian politics do not pass by State power, but rather by an immanent subjective determination, an axiom of the collective.

After all, from Plato and his unfortunate escapade in Sicily up to Heidegger's circumstantial aberrations, passing by the passive relationship between Hegel and Napoleon, and without forgetting Nietzsche's madness of pretending 'to split the history of the world in two', everything shows that it is not History on a large scale that authorizes philosophy. It is rather what Mallarmé called 'restrained action' ...

Let us be militants of restrained action. Let us be, within philosophy, those who eternalize the figure of such action.

We have too often wished that justice would act as the foundation for the consistency of the social bond, when it can only name the most extreme moments of inconsistency; for the effect of the egalitarian axiom is to undo bonds, to desocialize thought, and to affirm the rights of the infinite and the immortal against finitude, against being-for-death. Within the subjective dimension of the declaration of equality, nothing else is of interest save the universality of this declaration, and the active consequences to which it gives rise.

Justice is the philosophical name of the inconsistency, for the State or society, of any egalitarian political orientation. Here we can rejoin the poem in its declarative and axiomatic vocation, for it is Paul Celan who probably gives us the most exact image of what we must understand by 'justice':

On inconsistencies
Rest:
two fingers are snapping
in the abyss, a
world is stirring
in the scratch-sheets, it all depends
on you

Keep in mind the lesson of the poet: in matters of justice, where it is upon inconsistency that we must lean or rest, it is true, as true as a truth can be, that it all depends on you.

Note

1 This is a modified version of a translation by Thelma Sowley of 'Philosophie et politique', which appeared in *Radical Philosophy* 96 (July/August 1999), 29–32.

4
Philosophy and psychoanalysis

There is a psychoanalytic theory.[1] There is also a psychoanalytic practice, called the clinic. But what directly concerns the philosopher is neither the theory nor the practice. What concerns the philosopher is knowing whether psychoanalysis is a *thinking*.

I call thinking the non-dialectical or inseparable unity of a theory and a practice. To understand such a unity the simplest case is that of science; in physics there are theories, concepts and mathematical formulas and there are also technical apparatuses and experiments. But *physics* as a thinking does not separate the two. A text by Galileo or Einstein circulates between concepts, mathematics and experiments, and this circulation is the movement of a unique thinking.

Politics is also a thinking. Take the great political thinkers: Robespierre, Saint-Just, Lenin, Che Guevara, Mao. There you have concepts, theory, and even some philosophy. You also have fundamental writings: directives, commands and decisions. These writings are designed to concentrate the immanent relation between concepts and action. Finally you have treatments of concrete situations and their transformations. Here again, thinking circulates between theoretical hypotheses, statements and singular situations; and this thinking is a *unique* movement.

Psychoanalysis also presents itself as a thinking. In Lacan's case, everything can be found which is also found in physics: there are fundamental theoretical concepts, such as the Subject, the Ideal, the signifier, the Name-of-the-Father, etc. There are formalized writings such as the matheme for the fantasy, the formulas of sexuation or the Borromean knot. There is the clinical experience – the cure – which has precise rules, and there is even what could be called *experimental apparatuses*; for example, the protocol of the pass, invented by Lacan in 1967, and designed to verify the existence of an analytic act.[2]

What then becomes interesting for the philosopher is the comparison of psychoanalysis with other thinkings, such as science and politics. Of course, as practices, they are completely different. But that does not prevent the thinkings from having some characteristics in common. When is it that two thinkings have something in common? It is when the movement of thinking has the same structure. That is, when, *within the unity of the thinking* there is the same relation between *the moment of writing* and *the moment of transformation or experience*.

For example, science and politics are completely different thinkings. Why? Because in the science of physics the experiment is an artificial construction *which must be repeatable*. Mathematical writing corresponds to experiments solely when the repetition of an experiment gives the *same* result. This identity is inscribed in a mathematical equation. In politics, however, the relationship between writing and experience is completely different. A political situation is always singular; it is never repeated. Therefore political writings – directives or commands – are justified inasmuch as they inscribe, not a repetition, but, on the contrary, the *unrepeatable*. When the content of a political statement is a repetition, the statement is rhetorical and empty. It does not form part of a thinking. On this basis one can distinguish between *true political activists* and *politicians*. *True political activists* announce an unrepeatable possibility of a situation while a politician makes speeches based on the repetition of opinions. *True political activists* think *a* singular situation; politicians do not think.

The result is that political thinking is completely different to scientific thinking. Politics declares an irreducible and unrepeatable possibility. Science writes down a necessity and constructs apparatuses for a repetition.

What can be said of psychoanalytic thinking? What is certain is that in psychoanalysis the experience is not like that of science. It is a *clinical* experience which concerns a singular subject. Obviously one can say that no subject is ever the repetition of another. In psychoanalytic thinking, the relation between theoretical writing and the clinical situation is not established by the artificial construction of a repetition. One can thus say that psychoanalytic thinking resembles political thinking more than scientific thinking.

One sign of this resemblance between psychoanalysis and politics is the *necessity* for a collective organization of knowledge. That organization is necessary to politics is well known, as is the fact that there have always been associations of psychoanalysts. Why? It's simple: if the concrete situations dealt with are singular and unrepeatable, you can only verify your thinking in a subjective manner, by transmission to *others*.

In science there are two verifiable guarantees: the guarantee of mathematical demonstration, which can be reconstructed by anyone, and the guarantee of experiments, which can be repeated. Scientific thinking is ruled by repetition. What counts is the possibility of repetition. But what can be done when *there is no* repetition, neither demonstrative nor experimental? One must then *show* other people the relation between the statements or writings and the singular process. One must *rally* these others around a thinking, by referring to what does not repeat itself. An organization is thus necessary, in which one can discuss the assessment of unrepeatable experiences. What then counts is not the possibility of repetition; it is rather the possible thinking of what does not repeat itself. Moreover, one must obtain the *subjective* agreement of those with whom one is organized. They must recognize that there is indeed a thinkable relation between, on the one hand, your statements and writings, and on the other hand, the singularity of the clinic, in the case of psychoanalysis, or of action in the case of politics.

But is all this enough to say that political thinking and psychoanalytic thinking really resemble each other? In both cases there are theoretical statements or principles, unrepeatable situations, and collective organizations which validate the thinking. I believe, however, that there remains a great difference between the two.

In politics, thinking searches within a situation for a possibility *that the dominant state of things does not allow to be seen*. For example: today, in Europe as elsewhere, the state of things is the market economy, competition, the private sector, the taste for money, familial comfort, parliamentary elections, etc. A genuine political thinking will attempt to find a possibility which is *not* homogeneous with this state of things. A political thinking will say: here is a collective possibility; perhaps it is small and local, but its rule *is not* that of the dominant rule. And a political thinking will formulate this possibility, practise it, and draw all of its consequences. Political thinking always ruptures with the dominant state of things. In short, it ruptures with the State. And obviously, in order to do such work, one must *enter into the situation*, one must meet people and enter into discussion with them; one must exit from one's proper place. Political thinking demands a *displacement*, a journey which is always, dare I say, abnormal. For example, in May '68 and after in France, when the intellectuals went *en masse* to work in the factories, they embarked upon an absolutely abnormal journey in relation to the State. In doing so they created the conditions for an entirely new relation between the statements and the situations of politics.

Does the same thing happen in psychoanalysis? Well, the first thing one notices is that in psychoanalysis it is not the analyst who makes the journey – it is the analysand. Moreover, this journey is *fixed*. There is a place – the analyst's consulting rooms – there is a couch, and there are appointments to be kept. The second difference is that one must pay. This point is important because I am convinced that all genuine thinking is *free*. For example, one does not enter into politics to earn money, nor does one engage in politics to have a position, power, or privilege. Those who do so are politicians, but politicians do not think. Politics as thinking has no other objective than thinking; that is, no other objective than the transformation of unrepeatable situations – for in a thinking, there is no distinction between theory and practice. Politics is disinterested, exactly like science. Newton and Einstein's goal was to resolve the problems of thought and nothing more. This is also exactly like art: the goal of great artists is to give their thinking the form of a work, and nothing more. The goal of politics is to resolve political problems, problems that politics poses to itself. The question then arises of whether psychoanalysis is disinterested. Despite everything, yes. Freud's or Lacan's goal is not solely the client's cure. The goal is *to think* the singularity of the human subject: the human subject confronted on the one side with language, and, on the other, with sexuality.

But there is a problem which is still more profound. Political thinking searches for an active *possibility* which is not controlled by the State or by the blind laws of the economy. What does psychoanalytic thinking search for? What does it expect of the Subject? Does it search for an absolutely new possibility?

The Subject who comes into analysis is a suffering subject, suffering from his or her symptom. The stakes of the cure are primarily that the subject no longer suffers, or suffers less. But does this involve, as in politics, the *invention* of a possibility? Or rather solely a *displacement of the symptom*?

A true politics always situates itself in the faults or the impasses of a situation's structure. Of course, psychoanalysis also begins with disorders and symptoms. But politics searches for the most radical consequences of such disorders, and therefore works *against* structure: whereas it seems that psychoanalysis searches to reduce symptoms. Psychoanalysis thus works towards a 'normal' functioning of subjective structure.

As such, psychoanalytic thinking aims at the *Subject accommodating its real*. Whereas a political thinking aims at the exhaustion of a structure's – or a State's – ability to accommodate the point of the real worked by that political thinking. Perhaps what separates politics from psychoanalysis is this relation to the real. For psychoanalysis, the relation to the real is always finally inscribed in a structure. For politics the relation to the real is always subtracted from the State.

But perhaps all this is simply due to a difference of *matter*. What psychoanalysis aims to think is the *difference of the sexes*. The major thesis of psychoanalysis is: *There is no sexual relation*. Whence a negative figure which can be transformed into scepticism. What politics aims to think is the difference between collective presentation and State representation. Its major thesis: There is a possibility of pure presentation. Whence an affirmative figure which can be transformed into dogmatism.

The best solution would be the following: that political thinking protects itself from dogmatism by listening to psychoanalysis, and that psychoanalytic thinking protects itself from scepticism by listening to politics. After all, this is what Lacan authorizes us to do! In *Seminar XX* he compares the relation Lacan–Freud to the relation Lenin–Marx, whereby recognizing that the comparison of two thinkings is possible, and furthermore, that they may educate one another.[3]

But where can two different thinkings encounter each other? They can only do so in philosophy. The ultimate solution to our problem, the relation between psychoanalysis and politics, finally depends upon a philosophical choice.

Can one then attempt a direct comparison of psychoanalysis and philosophy?

The question which is formally common to both philosophy and psychoanalysis is without doubt the question of truth. It can be phrased as follows: How does a truth touch the real? For example, in November 1975 Lacan declares: 'Truth can only concern the real.' It is clear that philosophy and psychoanalysis have always asked themselves: What is truth such that it *only* concerns the real?

Psychoanalysis and contemporary philosophy have a point in common: they do not think that truth is correspondence or adequation between thought and the thing. For Heidegger, truth is unveiling. For Althusser, it is a ruled production. For myself, it is a process which is opened by an event and which constructs an infinite generic set. For Lacan, it is the depositing of speech in the Other. Thus truth is something other than a correct relationship between thought and object. In fact, for Lacan and for contemporary philosophy, thought is separated from the real. It has no direct access to, or acquaintance with this real. Let's say that between thought and the real there is a hole, an abyss, a void. The truth is first of all the effect of a separation, a loss, or a voiding.

For example, for Heidegger, truth occurs within a structure of forgetting. The history of truth is that of the forgetting of being. For myself, a truth commences by an event, but this event has always disappeared or been abolished; there will never be any knowledge of it. The event thus forms the real and absent cause of a truth. For Lacan, what founds truth is the Other as a hole in knowledge. Thus he declares, on 8 May 1973: 'There is a hole there and that hole is called the Other; the Other as place where speech, through being deposited, founds truth.'

Philosophy and psychoanalysis elaborate the same question: What is the thinkable relationship between truth and the void? The crux of the problem is the localization of the void. Philosophy and psychoanalysis agree that truth is separation; that the real is irreducible or, as Lacan says, unsymbolizable; that truth is different to knowledge, and that truth thus only occurs under condition of the void. It could be said that at base every theory consists of a localization of the void which authorizes truth, of its placement, and of the construction of its algebra and topology.

Thus for Heidegger, the void is thought as a figure of the Open. It is that for which poetry destines language. It is liberation from the violent will of technology which saturates and destroys our Earth. In Althusser's work there are two theories of the void. On the one hand, a structure only functions under the condition of an empty place. This is the theory of the causality of lack. On the other hand, philosophy itself uses empty categories because it is a pure act, an intervention. It traces lines of demarcation without ever knowing any object.

For myself the void is first of all the mathematical mark of being *qua* being, the void-set. It is what sutures mathematical discourse to pure presentation. Furthermore, the void is the destiny of any event, since the being of an event is a disappearing.

For Lacan, on the other hand, the void is not on the side of being. This, I think, is a crucial point of conflict. Let us say that philosophy localizes the void as condition of truth on the side of being *qua* being, while psychoanalysis localizes the void in the Subject, for the Subject is what disappears in the gap between two signifiers. It is on this basis that Lacan undertook the critique of philosophy or what he calls antiphilosophy. Why?

For Lacan, if the void is on the side of being, this means that thought is also on the side of being, because thought is precisely the exercise of separation. But on that basis one would say that being itself thinks. For Lacan the fundamental axiom of all philosophy is this idea that being thinks. I cite: 'The supposition that being thinks is what founds the philosophical tradition from Parmenides onwards.' For Lacan, this axiom is unacceptable. Thought must be an effect of the Subject, and not a supposition concerning being.

It appears that conflict is inevitable. The conflict concerns the triangle: Subject, Truth, Real. The topology of this triangle is different in philosophy and in psychoanalysis. However, this difference must be examined in detail. I will start with two statements by Lacan:

> 20 March 1973: The ideal of psychoanalysis is 'that, on the basis of its experience, a knowledge of truth can be constituted'.
> 15 May 1973: The core of his teaching is that 'there are some relations of being that cannot be known'. Or: 'Of what cannot be demonstrated, something true, however, can be said.'

There is a great difficulty here, a kind of contradiction. How can one obtain a 'knowledge of truth' if the content of that truth is precisely what cannot be known? How can a knowledge of the truth of the unknown exist? In psychoanalysis, what cannot be known ends up being the knowledge of a truth. This is clearly because what is not known consciously is known otherwise. Is it not, quite simply, because the unconscious thinks? But that the unconscious thinks, or, if you like, that 'it thinks', is this so different to the philosophical idea according to which being thinks?

In the end, to localize the void and truth, both philosophy and psychoanalysis need an axiom concerning thought.

The philosophical axiom: Thought must be understandable on the basis of being.

The psychoanalytic axiom: There is unconscious thought.

What the two have in common this time is that truth is torn away from consciousness; the effect of truth is thought outside conscious and reflexive production. This also means that the void is not that of consciousness: it is not Sartre's nothingness.

One very important consequence of this localization of the void outside consciousness is the importance of mathematics. Why? Because mathematics is precisely the thinking which has nothing to do with the experiences of consciousness; it is the thinking which has no relation to *reality*, but which knots *letters* and the *real* together; a thinking faced with the void because it obeys the ideal of formalization.

In fact, the veritable apparatus for the localization of the void is mathematics, because in its transmission, it entirely empties out what separates us from the real. Between the real and mathematical form there is nothing. This is why Lacan writes: 'Mathematical formalization is our goal, our ideal. Why? Because it alone is matheme, that is, capable of being transmitted in its entirety.' In the same manner, I posit that mathematics is the science of being *qua* being. And thus I would say, like Lacan, that mathematical formalization is compatible with our discourse, the philosophical discourse.

My proposition is the following: Psychoanalysis and philosophy have a common border; the ideal of the matheme. The real terrain for the examination of the relation between psychoanalysis and philosophy is found first of all in mathematics. There is no point in creating direct confrontations between the grand categories we share, such as being, the real, the subject, and truth. Rather what should be asked is: how do psychoanalysis and philosophy tackle the great constructions of mathematics and logic?

In fact, one can construct a list of questions that the psychoanalyst and the philosopher can discuss together. These are strange questions. For example:

Is there a relation between sexuation and opinions?
Is the philosophical idea of the One linked to the fantasy of the Woman?
Is the object cause of desire involved in the critical examination of the limits of truth?

Isn't the main obstacle to the death of God (as Nietzsche, moreover, thought) to be found on the side of feminine *jouissance* (enjoyment)? Could there be a philosophical thinking of the becoming-analyst, or of the pass?

Is there a logical subject?

But to guide these discussions in an ordered manner one must start from mathematics. Thus, to conclude, I would say that the common desire on the basis of which psychoanalysis and philosophy can enter into discussion is the desire of the matheme. It is quite a rare desire! This is why the discussion is also quite rare.

Notes

1   This paper was given in Melbourne in 1999 at the Australian Centre of Psychoanalysis. It was originally published in an earlier version of the same translation in the Centre's journal *Analysis* 9 (2000).
2   Translator's note: In French, the word *expérience* signifies both experiment and experience. This double signification should be kept in mind when either of the two English words occur.
3   J. Lacan, *Seminar XX Encore* (Paris: Editions du Seuil, 1989). All translations from *Encore* by Oliver Feltham unless noted.

5
Philosophy and art

Every philosophical enterprise turns back towards its temporal conditions in order to treat their compossibility at a conceptual level.[1] This turning back is clearly discernible in Heidegger's work, in four different modes.

1 The support taken from the intimate ek-stasis of time, from affect, from experience as filtered by the care of a question which directs its metamorphosis. This is the existential-ontological analysis of *Sein und Zeit*.
2 National-socialist politics, practised by Heidegger in a militant fashion as the German occurrence of resolute decision and of thought's engagement against the nihilist reign of technique, an engagement anchored in the categories of work, soil, community, and the appropriation of the site.
3 The hermeneutic and historial re-evaluation of the history of philosophy thought as the destiny of being in its coupling to the *logos*. Such are the brilliant analyses of Kant and Hegel, of Nietzsche and Leibniz, and then the lessons taken from the Greeks, singularly from the pre-Socratics.
4 The great German poems, seized from 1935 on, via the course on Hölderlin, as privileged interlocutors for the thinker.

This fourth support still survives today despite everything that managed to affect the three others. Its audience in France, including the poets, from René Char to Michel Deguy, is the strongest remaining validation of Heidegger's success in philosophically *touching* an unnoticed point of thought detained in poetic language. It is therefore indispensable, for whoever wishes to go beyond Heidegger's philosophical power, to reconsider the couple formed, in this philosophy's terms, by the saying of the poets and the thought of the thinker. The reformulation of that which both joins together and separates the poem and philosophical discursivity is an imperative which, thanks to Heidegger, we are obliged to submit ourselves to; whatever the avatars of his 'affair' may be.

Let us begin by recalling that, for Heidegger, there is an original *in*distinction between the two terms. In the pre-Socratic sending of thought, which is also the destinal sending of being, the *logos* is poetic as such. It is the poem that takes ward of thought, as we see in the *Poem* of Parmenides, or in the sentences of Heraclitus.

It is by a kind of axiomatic contestation of this point that I wish to begin the reconstruction of an *other relation*, or non-relation, between poetry and philosophy.

When Parmenides places his poem under the invocation of the Goddess, and begins with the image of an initiatory cavalcade, I think that it is necessary to maintain that this is not, that this is *not yet* philosophy. For every truth that accepts its dependence in regard to narrative and revelation is still detained in mystery; philosophy exists solely through its desire to tear the latter's veil.

The poetic form, with Parmenides, is essential; it covers with its authority the maintenance of discourse in the proximity of the sacred. However, philosophy can only begin by a desacralization: it institutes a regime of discourse which is its own earthly legitimation. Philosophy requires that the *profound* utterance's authority be interrupted by argumentative secularization.

Moreover it is at this very point that Parmenides provides a sort of pre-commencement of philosophy: in regard to the question of non-being, he sketches a reasoning by the absurd. This latent recourse to an autonomous rule of consistency is an interruption, within the poem, of the collusion organized by the poem between truth and the sacred authority of the image or story.

It is essential to see that the support for such an interruption can only be of the order of the matheme, if one understands by this the discursive singularities of mathematics. Apagogic reasoning is without doubt the most significant matrix of an argumentation that does not sustain itself on the basis of anything other than the imperative of consistency, and which turns out to be incompatible with any legitimation by narrative, or by the initiated status of the subject of the enunciation. Here, the matheme is that which, by causing the Speaker to disappear, by removing any mysterious validation from its site, exposes argumentation to the test of its autonomy and thus to the critical or dialogic examination of its pertinence.

Philosophy began in Greece because there alone the matheme allowed an interruption of the sacral exercise of validation by narrative (the mytheme, as Lacoue-Labarthe would say). Parmenides names the *pre-moment* – still internal to the sacred narrative and its poetic capture – of this interruption.

It is well known that Plato named this interruption himself, pushing reflection to a point of systematic suspicion towards anything reminiscent of the poem. Plato proposes a complete analysis of the gesture of interruption that constitutes the possibility of philosophy:

– As for the poem's imitative capture, its seduction without concept, its legitimation without Idea, it must be removed, banned from the space in which philosophy's royalty operates. This is a distressing, interminable rupture (see Book X of *The Republic*), but it is a question of the very *existence* of philosophy, and not solely of its style.
– The support that mathematics furnishes for the desacralization or depoetization of the truth must be explicitly sanctioned: pedagogically via the crucial place given to arithmetic and geometry in political education, and ontologically via their intelligible dignity which provides an antechamber to the ultimate deployments of the dialectic.

For Aristotle – as little a poet as is possible in his technique of exposition (Plato, on the other hand, and he recognizes it, is at every moment sensible to the charm of what he excludes) – the Poem is no longer anything but a particular object proposed to the dispositions of Knowledge; at the same time, moreover, that mathematics finds itself having all the attributes of ontological dignity accorded to it by Plato withdrawn. 'Poetics' is a regional discipline of philosophical activity. With Aristotle, the foundational debate is finished, and philosophy, stabilized in the connection of its parts, no longer turns back dramatically upon what conditions it.

Thus, from the Greeks onwards, *three possible regimes of the bond between the poem and philosophy* have been encountered and named.

1   The first, which we will call Parmenidian, organizes a *fusion* between the subjective authority of the poem and the validity of statements held as philosophical. Even when 'mathematical' interruptions figure under this fusion, they are definitively subordinated to the *sacred* aura of utterance, to its 'profound' value, to its enunciative legitimacy. The image, language's equivocations, and metaphor escort and authorize the saying of the True. Authenticity resides in the flesh of language.

2   The second, which we will call Platonic, organizes a *distance* between the poem and philosophy. The former is held to be separate as an undermining fascination, as a seduction which is diagonal to the True; the latter must disallow that what it deals with could be dealt with by poetry, *in its place*. The effort of uprooting from the prestige of poetic metaphor is such that support is required, support taken from what, in language, is opposed to poetic metaphor: the literal univocity of mathematics. Philosophy can only establish itself in the game of contrasts between the poem and the matheme, both its primordial conditions (the poem, whose authority it must interrupt, and the matheme, whose dignity it must promote). We can also say that the Platonic relation to the poem is a relation (negative) of *condition*, which implies other conditions (the matheme, politics, love).

3   The third, which we will call Aristotelian, organizes the *inclusion* of the knowledge of the poem within philosophy, itself representable as Knowledge of knowledges. The poem is no longer thought in terms of the drama of its distance or its intimate proximity; it is grasped *within the category of the object*, within what, in being defined and reflected as such, delimits a regional discipline within philosophy. This regionality of the poem founds what will be Aesthetics.

We can also say: the three possible relations of philosophy (as thought) to the poem are *identifying rivalry*, *argumentative distance* and *aesthetic regionality*. In the first case, philosophy wants the poem; in the second, it excludes it; and in the third, it categorizes it.

In regard to this triple disposition, what is the essence of the process of Heideggerean thought?

It can be schematized as having three components:

1   Heidegger has quite legitimately re-established the autonomous function of the thought of the poem. Or, more precisely, he has

sought to determine the place – a place itself withdrawn, or undetectable – from which the community of destiny between the conceptions of the thinker and the saying of the poet can be perceived. It could be said that this sketch of a community of destiny is primarily opposed to the third type of relation, that which is subsumed by an aesthetics of inclusion. Heidegger has subtracted the poem from philosophical *knowledge*, to render it to *truth*. By doing so, he has founded a radical critique of all aesthetics, of any regional philosophical determination of the poem. This foundation is established as a pertinent trait of modernity (its non-Aristotelian character).

2   Heidegger has shown the limits of a relation of condition that illuminates *solely* the separation of the poem and philosophical argument. In some sharp and distinctive analyses, he has established that, over a long period, from Hölderlin onwards, the poem acts in relay with philosophy with regard to essential themes, principally because for this entire period philosophy is captive either of the sciences (positivisms) or of politics (Marxisms). Philosophy is their captive just as we have said that in Parmenides it is still captive of the poem: it does not dispose, in regard to these particular conditions of its existence, of a sufficient game to establish its own law. I proposed calling this period the 'age of poets'.[2] Let us say that, investing this age with novel philosophical means, Heidegger showed that it was not always possible, nor just, to establish distance from the poem via the Platonic procedure of banishment. Philosophy is sometimes obliged to expose itself to the poem in a more perilous fashion: it must think for its own account of the *operations* by which the poem sets a date with a truth of Time (for the considered period, the principal truth poetically put to work is the destitution of the category of objectivity as necessary form of ontological presentation – whence the poetically crucial character of the theme of Presence; even, for example with Mallarmé, in its inverted form, isolation, or Subtraction).

3   Unfortunately, within his historial assemblage, and more particularly in his evaluation of the Greek origin of philosophy, Heidegger could not – for want of validating the *itself* originary character of the recourse to the matheme – but *renege on* the judgement of interruption, and restore, under various and subtle philosophical names, the sacral authority of the poetic utterance, and the idea that

the authentic lies in the flesh of language. There is a profound unity between, on the one hand, the recourse to Parmenides and Heraclitus considered as delimiting a site of pre-forgetting and the coming-forth of Being, and, on the other hand, the heavy and fallacious recourse to the sacred in the most contestable of the analyses of poems, especially the analyses of Trakl. The Heideggerean misunderstanding of the true nature of the Platonic gesture, at its core the misunderstanding of the mathematical sense of the Idea (which is precisely what, de-naturalizing it, exposes it to the withdrawal of Being), entails that instead of inventing a *fourth relation* between the philosopher and poem, neither fusional, nor distanced, nor aesthetic, Heidegger emptily prophesies a reactivation of the Sacred in an indecipherable coupling of the saying of poets and the thinking of thinkers.

We will retain from Heidegger the devaluation of all philosophical aesthetics and the critical limitation of the effects of the Platonic procedure of exclusion. We will contest, on the other hand, that it is again necessary, under conditions that would be those of the end of philosophy, to suture this end to the poem's authority without argument. Philosophy continues, inasmuch as positivisms are exhausted and Marxisms eviscerated, but also inasmuch as poetry itself, in its contemporary force, enjoins us to discharge it from every identifying rivalry with philosophy, and to undo it from the false couple of the saying of the poem and the thinking of the philosopher. For this couple of saying and thinking – forgetful of the ontological subtraction inaugurally inscribed by the matheme – is in fact that formed by the sermon of the end of philosophy and the romantic myth of authenticity.

That philosophy continues liberates the poem, the poem as a singular operation of truth. What would be the poem after Heidegger, the poem after the age of poets, the post-romantic poem? The poets will tell us, they have already told us, because to desuture philosophy and poetry, to leave Heidegger behind without returning to aesthetics, is also to think otherwise that from which the poem proceeds, thinking it in its operating distance, and not in its myth.

Two indications alone:

1   When Mallarmé writes: 'The moment of the Notion of an object is therefore the moment of the reflection of its pure present in itself or its present purity', what programme does he sketch for the poem, if it

is attached to the *production* of the Notion? It will be a question of determining by which operations internal to language one can make a 'present purity' *arise*; that is, the separation, the isolation, the coldness of that which is only present insofar as it no longer has any presentable relation to reality. One could maintain that poetry *is* the thought of the presence of the present. And that it is precisely because of this that it is not in rivalry with philosophy, which has as its stake the compossibility of Time, and not pure presence. Only the poem accumulates the means of thinking outside-place, or beyond all place, 'on some vacant and superior surface', what of the present does not let itself be reduced to its reality, but summons the eternity of its presence: 'A Constellation, icy with forgetting and desuetude.' Presence that, far from contradicting the matheme, *also* implies 'the unique number that cannot be another'.

2   When Celan tells us,

> Wurfscheibe, mit
> Vorgesichten besternt,
> wirf dich
> aus dir hinaus.

which can be translated as,

> Cast-disc, with
> Foreseeings bestarred,
> cast yourself
> out your outside.

what is the intimacy of this intimation? It can be understood in the following manner: when the situation is saturated by its own norm, when the calculation of itself is inscribed there without respite, when there is no longer a void between knowledge and prediction, then one must be *poetically* ready for the outside-of-self. For the nomination of an event – in the sense in which I speak of it, that is, an undecidable supplementation which must be named to occur for a being-faithful, thus for a truth – *this* nomination is *always* poetic. To name a supplement, a chance, an incalculable, one must draw from the void of sense, in default of established significations, to the peril of language. One must therefore poeticize, and the poetic name of the event is what throws us outside of ourselves, through the flaming ring of predictions.

The poem freed from philosophical poeticizing; undoubtedly it will have always been these two thoughts, these two donations: the presence of the present in the transfixion of realities, the name of the event in the leap outside calculable interests.

Nonetheless, we can and we must, we philosophers, leave to the poets the care of the future of poetry beyond all that the hermeneutic concern of the philosopher pressed upon it. Our singular task is rather to rethink, from the point of philosophy, its liaison or its un-liaison with the poem, in terms that can be neither those of the Platonic banishment, nor those of the Heideggerean suture, nor even those of the classificatory care of an Aristotle or a Hegel. What is it which, in the act of philosophy as in its style of thought, is found from the very origin under the condition of the poem, at the same time as under that of the matheme, or politics, or love? Such is our question.

The moderns, even more so, the postmoderns, have willingly exposed the wound which would be inflicted upon philosophy by the unique mode in which poetry, literature, art in general, bear witness to our modernity. There will always have been a challenge laid down by art to the concept, and it is on the basis of this challenge, this wound, that it is necessary to interpret the Platonic gesture which can only establish the royalty of the philosopher by banishing the poets.

To my mind, there is nothing in such a gesture that is specific to poetry or literature. Plato also has to hold philosophical love, *philosophia*, at a distance from real love gripped in the malaise of a desire for an object. He also has to hold real politics at a distance, that of Athenian democracy, in order to fashion the philosophical concept of *politeia*. He must equally affirm the distance and the supremacy of the dialectic in regard to mathematical *dianoia*. Poem, matheme, politics and love at once condition and insult philosophy. Condition and insult: that's the way it is.

Philosophy wants to and must establish itself at this subtractive point where language consecrates itself to thought without the prestige and the mimetic incitements of the image, fiction or narrative; where the principle of amorous intensity unbinds itself from the alterity of the object and sustains itself from the law of the Same; where the illumination of the Principle pacifies the blind violence that mathematics assumes in its axioms and its hypotheses; where, finally, the collective is represented in its symbol, and not in the excessive real of political situations.

Philosophy is under the conditions of art, science, politics and love, but it is always damaged, wounded, serrated by the evental and singular character of these conditions. Nothing of this contingent occurrence pleases it. Why?

To explain this displeasure of philosophy with regard to the real of its conditions presumes that one sets at the heart of its disposition the following, that truth is distinct from sense. If philosophy had only to *interpret* its conditions, if its destiny was hermeneutic, it would be pleased to turn back towards these conditions, and to interminably say: such is the sense of what happens in the poetic work, the mathematical theorem, the amorous encounter, the political revolution. Philosophy would be the tranquil aggregate of an aesthetics, an epistemology, an erotology and a political sociology. This is a very old temptation, which, when one cedes to it, classifies philosophy in a section of what Lacan calls the discourse of the University.

But 'philosophy' begins when this aggregate turns out to be inconsistent, when it is no longer a question of interpreting the real procedures where truth lies, but of founding a unique place in which, under the contemporary conditions of these procedures, it may be stated how and why a truth is not a sense, being rather a *hole in sense*. This 'how' and this 'why', founders of a place of thought under conditions, are only practicable in the displeasure of a refusal of donation and of hermeneutics. They require the primordial defection of the donation of sense, ab-sense, abnegation in regard to sense. Or rather, indecency. They require that truth procedures be subtracted from the evental singularity that weaves them in the real, and that knots them to sense in the mode of traversing the latter, of hollowing it out. They thus require that truth procedures be disengaged from their subjective escort, including the pleasure of the object delivered there.

As such philosophy will:

– Envisage love according to the truth alone that weaves itself upon the Two of sexuation, and upon the Two quite simply. But without the tension of pleasure/displeasure that sustains itself from the object of love.
– Envisage politics as truth of the infinity of collective situations, as a treatment *in truth* of this infinity, but without the enthusiasm and the sublimity of these situations themselves.
– Envisage mathematics as truth of multiple-being in and by the letter,

> the power of literalization, but without the intellectual beatitude of the resolved problem.
> – Envisage finally the poem as truth of sensible presence deposited in rhythm and image, but without the corporeal captation by this rhythm and this image.

What causes the constitutive displeasure of philosophy with regard to its conditions, with the poem as with the others, is having to *depose*, along with sense, whatever *jouissance* (enjoyment) is determined there, at the very point where a truth occurs as a hole in the knowledges that make sense.

Being more particularly a question of the literary act, whose kernel is the poem; what is the forever offended and recalcitrant procedure of this deposition?

The relation is all the more narrow since philosophy is an effect of language. The literary is specified for philosophy as fiction, as comparison, image or rhythm, and as narrative.

The deposition takes here the figure of a *placement*.

Certainly, philosophy uses fictive incarnations in the texture of its exposition; hence the characters of Plato's dialogues, and the staging of their encounters, or the conversation of a Christian philosopher and an improbable Chinese philosopher with Malebranche.[3] Or the at once epic and novelistic singularity of Nietzsche's Zarathustra, kept so much in the fiction of character that Heidegger is able to ask, in a text which is perhaps a little too hermeneutic: 'Who is Nietzsche's Zarathustra?'

Philosophy uses image, comparison and rhythm. The image of the sun serves to expose to the day of presence that there is something essentially *withdrawn* in the Idea of the Good. And who doesn't know the marvellous paragraph 67 of Leibniz's *Monadology*, filled with cadences and alliterations: 'each portion of matter may be conceived as a garden full of plants, and like a pond full of fish. But each branch of the plant, each member of the animal, each drop of its humours is again such a garden or such a pond'?

Finally, philosophy uses the narrative, the fable and the parable. The myth of Er closes Plato's *Republic*. Hegel's philosophy of History is in many respects the monumental narrative and recitation of those great subjective entities that are named the Orient, Greece, or Rome. And 'Zarathustra, dying, holds the earth embraced.'

Nonetheless, these occurrences of the literary as such are placed under the jurisdiction of a principle of thought that they do not constitute. They are *localized* in points at which – in order to complete the establishment of the place in which why and how a truth hollows sense and escapes interpretation is stated – one must precisely, through a paradox of exposition, propose a fable, an image or a fiction to interpretation itself.

Philosophy has subtracted from the truth procedures that condition it all *aura* of sense, all trembling and all pathos, to seize *truth's proving of itself* as such. But there is a moment where it falls on the radical underside of all sense, the void of all possible presentation, the hollowing of truth as a hole *without borders*. This moment is that in which the void, ab-sense – such as philosophy ineluctably encounters them at the point of truth's proving of itself – must be themselves presented and transmitted.

The poem occurs in philosophy when the latter, in its will to universal address, in its vocation to make the place that it erects inhabited by all, falls under the imperative of having to propose to sense and to interpretation the latent void that sutures all truth to the being of that of which it is truth. This presentation of the unpresentable void requires the deployment within language of the latter's literary resources; but under the condition that it occur at this very point; thus under the general jurisdiction of an entirely different style, that of argumentation, of conceptual liaison, or of the Idea.

The poem occurs in philosophy *at one of its points*, and this localization is never ruled by a poetic or literary principle. It depends on the moment at which the argument places the unpresentable, and where, by a torsion prescribed by the argument, the nudity of the operations of the true is only transmissible by a return, always immoderate, to the pleasure of sense, which is always also a pleasure of the senses. The literary in philosophy is the directed transmission, the vectoring, through an effect of sense, of the following: the relation of a truth to sense is a defective or void relation. It is this defection that exposes philosophy to the imperative of a localized fiction. The moment at which the argumentation fails imitates, amid the power of the argument itself, this, that truth causes the failure of knowledge.

It is hardly astonishing that in these conditions the greatest known philosophical poem is that of an author for whom the Void as such is the original principle for an intransigent materialism. Evidently Lucretius is the philosopher in question. For Lucretius, all truth establishes itself from a combination of marks, from a rain of letters, atoms, in the pure unpresentable that is the void. This philosophy is particularly subtracted from sense, particularly disappointing for the *jouissance* of interpretation. Moreover, it cannot be incorporated into the Heideggerean schema of metaphysics. Nothing in it is ontotheological; there is no supreme being for Lucretius, the heaven is void, the gods are indifferent. Is it not remarkable that the only thinker who is also an immense poet be precisely the one who causes the Heideggerean historical assemblage to default, the one who takes the history of being through a disseminated multiplicity foreign to everything that Heidegger tells us of metaphysics since Plato? Is it not symptomatic that this singular fusion of poem and philosophy, unique in history, be precisely that which is entirely foreign to the schema through which Heidegger thinks the correlation of the poem and thought? Nevertheless, it is this materialist, neuter thought, entirely orientated towards the deposition of the imaginary, hostile to any unanalysed effect of presence, which requires, in order to expose itself, the prestige of the poem.

Lucretius sustains philosophy by the poem all the way through, for the very reason that apparently ought to engage him in a banishment of the Platonic type. Because his only principle is material dissemination. Because it exposes as place for the proving of the true the most radical defection of sacred bonds.

At the beginning of Book 4 of *De rerum natura*, which one should translate by 'Of the real of being-multiple', Lucretius undertakes, against Plato if you like, to legitimate the poem as the expository imperative of his philosophy. What are his arguments? There are principally three.

First, the book treats, Lucretius says, of an 'obscure thing'. And the presentation of this obscurity of being requires light in and by language, the luminous verses of the poem: *'obscura de re tam lucida pango carmina'*.

Next, Lucretius sets himself to disengage spirit from the tight bonds of religion. In order to operate this unbinding, this subtraction from the sense that religion continually pours out, what is necessary is a force of saying, a prestige, such as lavished upon us by the graces of the Muse.

Finally, the bare truth, anterior to the occupation of its place, essentially appears sad. The philosophical place, the place of the occurrence, or the proving ground of the true, when seen *from a distance*, is, for most people, melancholic. This deposition of pleasure must be sustained by a supernumerary and lateral pleasure, that lavished by the finery, Lucretius says, of 'sweet poetic honey'.

Thus the poem, this time, reopens the entire philosophical exposition, the entire philosophical address *to* the universal occupation of its site. It does this under the triple injunction of the melancholy of truths seen from a distance, or, says Lucretius, 'not yet practised'; of the unbinding, or subtraction of sense, that obliterates religion; and finally of the obscure, whose heart is the unpresentable void, that occurs within transmission via the razing light of its glorious linguistic body.

However, that which, in these injunctions, strictly maintains the gap between philosophy and poetry remains. Because language (*la langue*) and the charm of verse are only there in the position of supplement. They escort the will of the transmission. They are thus still and always localized, prescribed. The real law of the discourse remains constructive and rational argument, such as Lucretius receives from Epicurus. Lucretius explains why he has recourse to the poem; it is almost an excuse, and its referent is he to whom one addresses oneself, who must be persuaded that the sadness of the true seen from a distance changes into the joy of being when seen close up. When it is a question of Epicurus, what is required is no longer legitimation, but pure and simple praise. The poem must be excused, the argument must be praised. The gap remains, essential.

This is because the poem exposes itself as imperative in language, and, in doing so, *produces* truths. Philosophy does not produce any. It supposes and subtractively distributes them according to their proper regime of separation from sense. Philosophy only summons the poem for itself at the point at which this separation must expose what the argument, which frames and borders it, can only sustain by returning to what made it possible: the effective singularity of a truth procedure, singularity that is in the bathing pool, in the winding sheet, in the source of sense.

The poem is summoned by philosophy when the latter must *also* say, in Lucretius' expression: 'I voyage through unvisited places in the domain of the Pierides, never before trodden. I love to go and draw water from virgin springs.'

The poem marks the moment of the empty page in which the argument proceeds, proceeded, will proceed. This void, this empty page, is not 'all is thinkable'. It is, on the contrary, under a rigorously circumscribed poetic mark, the means of saying, in philosophy, that at least one truth, elsewhere, but real, exists, and drawing from this recognition, against the melancholy of those who regard from afar, the most joyful consequences.

Notes

1 Translator's note: This chapter was published as 'Le Recours philosophique au poème', in A. Badiou, *Conditions* (Paris: Seuil, 1992), 93–107. 'Compossibility' is a term drawn from Leibniz, meaning common or shared possibility.

2 I proposed the category of an 'age of poets' for the first time in my *Manifesto for Philosophy* (New York: SUNY Press 1999).

3 The obvious reference here is Deleuze and Guattari's brilliant analysis of the 'conceptual character' in *What is Philosophy?*, trans. G. Burchell and H. Tomlinson (London: Verso, 1994), posterior to the current essay. However, the distance should be remarked. In my conception, philosophical theatrality designates the following: the essence of philosophy (the seizure 'in Truth') is an act. For Deleuze and Guattari, as always, everything is referred to movement and description: the conceptual character is the nomad on the plane of immanence.

6
Philosophy and cinema

1   On the notion of 'the situation of cinema'

There is no 'objective' situation of cinema. That is, the situation of cinema – or, the current conjuncture of this artistic procedure – cannot be situated 'in itself'. 'What is happening' (the films which are released) does not produce, on its own, any sort of intelligibility. There are general reasons behind this lack, but there are also reasons linked to the singularity of the cinematographic procedure.

(a) General reasons

The relation of thought to the current moment in art is one of a localized prescription and not a description. Everything depends upon the point at which one is subjectively situated, and upon the axioms which are used to support judgements. The point at which we choose to situate ourselves is called *L'Art du Cinéma*, which claims a local status quite different to that of a simple review: a group of thought, possessing an orientation and particular protocols for enquiry.[1] It possesses two foundational axioms; drawn from Denis Levy's work:

1   Cinema is capable of being an art, in the precise sense in which one can identify, among the undividedness of forms and subjects, cinema-ideas.
2   This art has been traversed by a major rupture, between its identificatory, representative and humanist ('Hollywoodian') vocation and a modernity which is distanced, involving the spectator in an entirely different manner.

The 'current situation of cinema' (or conjuncture) can then be called the legibility of an indistinct real (films which are made) on the basis of two axioms. One can then produce derived propositions, or propositions of the situation. These propositions identify the situation, not 'objectively', but on the basis of engagements concerning something which has recognizable artistic autonomy. This is a little like parliamentary politics, in a given situation, only being identifiable on the basis of the statements of the *Organisation politique*.[2]

In what follows what must not be forgotten is that it is the films of Oliveira, of Kiarostami, of Straub, of the early Wenders, of a certain Pollet, of some Godards, etc., which prescribe the conjuncture, or which provide the measure for derived judgements. They are what allow us to identify everything in the situation which is relatively progressive from the standpoint of art, even when this progressivism occurs within frameworks or references foreign to what *L'Art du Cinéma* terms modernity. They also provide the measure of the new, precisely because they were the new. The new does not enter into a dialectic with the old, but rather with the old new, or the new of the preceding sequence.

(b) Particular reasons

The latter are attached to a thesis which has been incorporated into *L'Art du Cinéma*'s doctrine; that of the essential impurity of cinema. Up till the present, this thesis has signified above all that the passage of an idea in a film presupposes a complex summoning forth and displacement of the other arts (theatre, the novel, music, painting . . .), and that as such 'pure cinema' does not exist, except in the dead-end vision of avant-garde formalism. This thesis of impurity must be expanded: the following principle should be proposed; the cinema is a place of intrinsic indiscernibility between art and non-art. No film, strictly speaking, is controlled by artistic thinking from beginning to end. It always bears absolutely impure elements within it, drawn from ambient imagery, from the detritus of other arts, and from conventions with a limited shelf life. Artistic activity can only be discerned in a film as a *process of purification of its own immanent non-artistic character*. This process is never completed. Even better, if it was completed, thereby generating the supposed purity of experimental cinema (or even certain radical normative statements by Bresson on 'cinematographic writing'), then the artistic capacity itself, or rather, its universal address, would be suppressed. Cinema's artistic operations are incompletable purification operations, bearing on current non-artistic forms, or indistinct imagery (Rimbaud's 'idiotic paintings').

The result of all this is that the dominant forms of non-art are immanent to art itself, and make up part of its intelligibility. Hence the permanent necessity of enquiry into the dominant formal tendencies within current production, and of the identification of circulating, even industrial, schemas of the visible and the audible; because it is upon the latter that artistic operations are potentially performed.

2 Four examples

(a) The Godardian technique of 'dirty sound' (inaudible phrases, super-imposition of sounds, parasitical noises, etc.) is an attempt at a formal purification of what has invaded contemporary production; that is, the constant confusion of music (in its post-rock form), brutal sounds (arms, explosions, cars, planes, etc.) and dialogues reduced to their operational ineptness. In current production, there is an imposition of sound, or a submission to the demand, characteristic of contemporary youth, for a permanent rhythmic background accompanying every activity, even speech or writing: this is what Godard transforms into an adulterated murmur. By means of this operation, what Godard does is treat the confusion of the world as artifice, as voluntary principle of the confusion of thoughts.

(b) The usage of car sequences in Kiarostami or even Oliveira's films works on an overwhelming stereotype of contemporary imagery, thanks to which the opening scene of two films out of every three is a car sequence. The operation consists of making an action scene into the place of speech, of changing what is a sign of speed into a sign of slowness, of constraining what is an exteriority of movement to become a form of reflexive or dialogic interiority.

(c) Sexual activity, filmed directly on bodies, forms a major part of what is authorized by dominant contemporary imagery. It is opposed to the metonymy of desire, which was one of the key characteristics of classic cinematographic art, and which aimed at avoiding the censor by sexualizing tiny details. The artistic problem is thus: what usage can be made of sexualized nudity in its tendentiously full exposition? The attempts at purifying such material are innumerable; whether they turn it towards speech (in contemporary French comedy), or ritualize it (certain of Antonioni's sequences), or make distanced citations of it, or render it banal by incorporating it into a genre (as Eastwood does in *The Bridges of Madison County*), or overpornographize it in an abstract manner (Godard at times).

(d) Special effects of any kind, the formalized spectacle of destruction, of cataclysm, a sort of Late Roman Empire consummation of murder, cruelty and catastrophe: these are the obvious ingredients of current cinema. They are inscribed in a proven tradition, but there is no longer much of an attempt to embed them in a consistent fable with a moral, indeed religious, vocation. They derive from a technique of shock and one-upmanship, which is related to the end of an epoch in which images were relatively rare and it was difficult to obtain them. The endless discussions about the 'virtual' and the image of synthesis refer to nothing other than the overabundance and facility of the image, including the spectacularly catastrophic or terrorizing image. Here again, attempts at purification exist, directed towards a stylized inflation, a type of slowed calligraphy of general explosion; the grand master evidently being John Woo.

3   A thesis and its consequences

One can then formulate the following principle: *A film is contemporary, and thus destined for everyone, inasmuch as the material whose purification it guarantees is identifiable as belonging to the non-art of its times.*

This is what makes cinema, intrinsically and not empirically, into a mass art: its internal referent is not the artistic past of forms, which would suppose an educated spectator, but a common imagery whose filtering and distancing treatment is guaranteed by potential artistic operations. Cinema gathers around identifiably non-artistic materials, which are ideological indicators of the epoch. It then *transmits*, potentially, their artistic purification, within the medium of an apparent indiscernibility between art and non-art.

Whence, to think the current situation of cinema, a number of directions for our enquiry:

(a) Of course, we will maintain the idea that the artistic operations of modernity consist in purifying visible and audible materials of everything which binds them to the domination of representation, identification and realism. But we will add that the current challenge is that of extending this treatment to everything which binds the materials to the pure formal consumption of images and sounds, whose privileged operators today are: pornographic nudity, the cataclysmic special effect, the intimacy of the couple, social melodrama, and pathological cruelty. For it is only by purifying these operators, while recognizing their necessity, that one gives oneself the chance of encountering a real *in situation*, and thus of assuring the passage, or the visitation, of a new cinema-idea.

(b) What is thus required is knowledge of materials in their real movement, and knowledge of the dominant tendencies which organize the latter.

(c) Cinematic works must be dealt with and hypotheses of configuration made: this on the basis of the operations of purification and displacement of materials and their operators; operations through which cinema-ideas will occur which are effectively contemporary and which have a universal address.

At this point in time, it is quite probable that the basic unit of investigation is not so much a film in its totality as some moments of film, moments within which an operation is legible. Legibility means the following: one grasps, at the same time, the subjacent material, which assures that the film is contemporary, the protocol of purification, which is the artistic index, and the passage of the idea (or encounter with a real), which is the effect of the protocol. In the current phase of transition, within which the weight of non-art is crushing (because, and we will come back to this, in general, nothing else is opposed to it apart from a formalized distance), it is necessary to engage in the work of identification of operations including those occurring within films which are globally deficient. In this work we will not be entirely guided by the notion of *auteur*, because, no doubt, nobody as yet maintains a mastered and consistent relation to the mutation of material (what is it to make films when every image is *facile*?). If such a relation emerged, then we would have a great *mass auteur* on our hands, such as Chaplin or Murnau, and without a doubt we would have such within a determined genre born from the situation. Yet nothing of the sort is on the horizon, neither in explosive neo-thrillers (despite the existence of auteurs of quality such as Woo or de Palma), nor in gore films (despite Craven's subtle displacements), nor in pornography (Bénazéraf has not kept any of his promises), nor in social melodrama (despite the efforts of a few English filmmakers).

There is thus a necessity for an enquiry into the details, guided by the sense of possible situations, by our 'consumerist' visits to the cinema (to a certain degree we should share in the innocent fairground mass aspect of 'seeing films'), by our instinct, and by the decoding of current criticism.

4 Exceptions

One should set apart the cases in which, for a certain period of time, a vast political modification, a global event, authorized the discredit of ordinary industrial materials (let us say Hollywoodian materials, or Indian, or Egyptian), and made possible an original grasp of the evental site. During at least one temporal sequence, the cinema's mass dimension was incompatible with a direct concern to invent forms in which the real of a country occurs as a problem. This was the case in Germany, as the escort of leftism (Fassbinder, Schroeter, Wenders ...), in Portugal after the 1975 revolution (Oliveira, Botelho ...), and in Iran after the Islamic revolution (Kiarostami ...). In all of these examples it is clear that what cinema is capable of *touches* the country, as a subjective category (what is it to be from this country?). There are cinema-ideas concerning this point, such as its previous invisibility is revealed by the event. A national cinema with a universal address emerges; a national *school*, recognizable in everything up to its insistence on certain formal aspects.

5 Formal operators and dominant motifs

Besides national exceptions, the enquiry must determine the situation with regard to conclusive operations practised upon a certain number of dominant motifs, more or less coded within genres. What virtual ideas are at work in these operations?

(a) The visibility of the sexual, or, more generally, the motif of erogenous nudity. The question is that of knowing what this motif, purified, but without any possibility of a return to the classical metonymies imposed by censorship, can bring to bear concerning the non-relation between love and sexuality. Or how can it prove an exception (when first of all it confirms it) to the contemporary subsumption of love by the functional organization of enjoyment. What degree of visibility can be tolerated by what one could call the amorous body? A simple critical analysis of pornography is only the first stage, as can be seen in Godard's abstract pornographic scenes, for example in *Sauve qui peut (la vie)*. As yet no conclusive work has been done on this point, and the identification of some attempted operations upon this motif would be welcome.

A subsidiary question would be that of asking oneself whether pornography, X movies, could become a genre. Let us agree that what is termed 'genre' has given rise to artistic enterprises. Otherwise, one can speak of specialities. Is pornography necessarily a speciality and not a genre? And if so, why? This is a particularly interesting question with regard to the very essence of cinema insofar as it is confronted with the full visibility of the sexual.

(b) Extreme violence, cruelty. This is a complex zone, which includes the theme of the torturing serial killer (*Seven*), and its horror gore variations (*Halloween, Scream . . .*), the violent neo-thriller, certain films about the mafia (even *Casino* contained shots of an unmeasured cruelty), and films about the end of the world with various tribal survivors cutting each other's throats. It is not a matter of variations of the horrifying film as a genre. The element of cruelty, the slashing, the crushing of bones, the torture, prevails over suspense and fear. It is an ensemble which actually evokes the late Roman Empire, because its essential material consists of its variations on putting-to-death.

The point is one of knowing whether all this could be exposed to a *tragic* treatment. Before judging these bloody torturing images, one must remember that tales of horrendous executions, the variety of murders, and the monstrosity of actions, were all major elements of the most refined tragedies. All one has to do is reread the tale of Hyppolite's death in Racine's *Phaedrus*. After all, one can hardly better the Greek story of Atreus and Thyestes, a major narrative commonplace in tragedy in which one sees a father eat his own children. Here, our enquiry is guided by a simple question: do embryonic operations exist which announce that all this material – which acts like an urban mythology for today – will be integrated into attempts at contemporary baroque tragedy?

(c) The figure of the worker. It is well known that there has recently been a return, via England, but also in American documentaries, of social melodrama. Even in France, all sorts of attempts, from *Reprise* to *Marius et Jeanette*, aim at giving a verdict on a certain figure of the worker, in the milieu of the PCF or May '68.[3] The problem is then one of knowing whether cinema can contribute to the subjective generalization of the autonomy of the figure of the worker. For the moment the cinema only deals with the latter's end, and as such gives rise to nostalgic operations, like those of *Brassed Off*.

The history of this question is very complex, if one thinks simultaneously of *Modern Times* (Chaplin), of French noir romanticism (*Le Jour se lève*), of the epic Soviet films, and of the films of the sequence opened by '68 (*Tout va bien, Oser lutter* ...). Today the question would be: What is the formal operator which purifies this figure's passage of all nostalgia, and contributes to its *installation*? That is, to its detachment from any social objectivity? What is at stake is the very possibility of a real encounter of cinema and politics; no doubt the figure of the worker would have to be the film's unfigurable real point – much as it is sketched, after all, in Denis Levy's *L'Ecole de Mai* (1979).

(d) The millenarian motif. This occurs in the register of planetary catastrophes from which some yankee hero saves us. The subjacent real is globalization, the hegemony of one sole superpower, and also ecological ideologies concerning the global village and its survival. The fundamental imagery is that of the catastrophe, and not that of salvation. Moreover, this 'genre' already comes with its own ironic version (see *Mars Attacks*). The point lies in knowing whether the motif of a general threat can provide the material for an operation which would transmit the idea that the world is prey to Capital in its unbridled form, and by this very fact rendered, globally, foreign to the very truths that it detains in its midst. This time it is clear that it is the possibility of an epic film which is at stake, but of an epic whose 'hero' is restricted action, truth procedures' confidence in themselves.

(e) The petit-bourgeois comedy. Here we have a highly prized modern variation of the French intimist tradition. The comedy revolves around a young hystericized woman, of a certain vacuity, who is fraught by her amorous, social and even intellectual wanderings. As such, this genre is linked to Marivaux and Musset, as it is to the Marianne of *Caprices*, and given its clear delineation in the work of its founding father, Rohmer. Almost all recent French 'auteurs' have been involved in this business. It is still a minor genre with regard to the American comedy of the 1930s and 40s, which is similar in many respects, termed by Stanley Cavell the comedy of 'remarriage'.

Why such minor inferiority? We should be able to respond to this question. For example, it could be said that the central weakness of these films is that the central stakes of the intrigue remain undetermined. In the American films as in Marivaux there is a decision or a declaration at the end of the day. The comedy of uncertainty and the double game is articulated around this fixed point. This is what allows Marivaux's prose to be simultaneously underhand and extremely firm. If Rohmer remains superior to his descendants, it is because among his Christian allusions to grace, he occasionally finds something which is at stake. In *Conte d'Automne* it is obvious that the main motif is: 'Happier are the simple of mind, the grace of love is reserved for them.' Nothing of the sort is to be found in the work of a Desplechin, a Barbosa or a Jacquot. In the end, this genre only gains artistic force when it gives itself, on the basis of an unshakeable confidence in love's capacities, a fixed point, such as required by all comedies in order to tie down their internal wanderings.

Psychoanalysis, made much use of by current auteurs (including the sad Woody Allen), is a dead end, because, paradigmatically, it is the place of the interminable.

We can no longer symbolize the fixed point by marriage or even remarriage. No doubt, as Rohmer suggests, and sometimes Téchiné, it is to be found where love encounters another truth procedure. It would then be necessary to formalize a subjective ex-centring, a conversion, a visible distancing, and finally, a displacement with regard to the dominant conception, even if the latter serves as initial material, a conception which is a mix of narcissism and hystericized inertia.

6   Cinema and the other arts

The generalization of the notion of impurity must not cause us to forget that it is first of all an impurity with regard to other arts. What are the contemporary forms of this question?

(a) On cinema and music. The schema must be drawn up on the basis of rhythm. We will call 'rhythm' not exactly the characteristics of the editing, but a diffused temporality which fixes, even if it is a matter of a sequence shot, the tonality of the movement (staccato, or hurried, or expanded, or slow and majestic, etc. ...). Rhythm engages every element of the film, and not only the organization of shots and sequences. For example, the style of acting or the intensity of the colours contribute to rhythm just as much as the speed of the succession of shots. At base, rhythm is the general pulsation of filmic transitions. Music is a type of immediate commentary upon the latter, often purely redundant or emphatic. Yet it is clearly rhythm which ties cinema to music.

The twentieth century, which, after all, was the century of cinema, essentially witnessed three types of music. First, there was post-romantic music which maintained the artifices of the finishing tonality, such as found in Mahler or Tchaikovsky's symphonic melancholy, and which continues, via Strauss or Rachmaninov, right through to the current day, and singularly in cinema. Second, the great creation of American blacks, jazz, which has its major artists from Armstrong to Monk, but to which we must also attach, in mass, everything which falls under the term 'youth music', from rock to techno. Finally, there was a continuation through rupture of veritable musical creation, which, from Schoenberg to Brian Ferneyhough, liquidated tonality and constructed a universe of musical singularities, serial and post-serial.

At the cinema, we have watched a massive movement, as yet incomplete (because every neo-classical film reclassicizes music), from post-romantic music to post-jazz music. This accompanies, at the level of rhythm, a passage from an emphatic aesthetic of dilation (taken to its extreme in the openings of Westerns, which are genuinely symphonic) to an aesthetic of fragmentation, whose matrix, as everyone remarks, is the video clip, a sub-product of youth-music.

The central problem seems to be the following: could a rhythm be invented which would tie cinema to the real of music as art, and not to the decomposed forms of symphonism or the demagogic forms of youth music? How is it possible that cinema has left aside the entirety of contemporary musical creation? Why, besides post-romanticism and post-jazz, isn't there a cinema of post-serial music? Do we not have here – it being a matter, after all, of what has been, for a century, genuine music – one of the reasons which – cinema being the essential mass art – relegates the sole restrained action of musical creation to the shadows? We must return to the few attempts at filmic and thus rhythmic incorporation of the music of our times, in Straub or Oliveira's work, in order to discern the operations which make a strength out of it, but which have also limited it.

(b) On cinema and theatre. *L'Art du Cinéma* has spent a lot of time working on this question. In order to progress further the best question to be asked is probably the following: What is a cinematic actor today? This is a question which traverses all the other questions. Today, an American actor is dominated by the imperative of sexual visibility, by confrontation with extreme violence and by millenarian heroism. He is an immobile receptacle for a type of disintegrating cosmos. He alone bears the latter's consistency, or what remains of it. In the end, he forms a type of invulnerable body. Moreover, this is why the actor is essentially a man, an impassive athlete. Women are almost uniformly decorative, far more so now than in the previous epoch, during which they were able to occupy the pernicious centre of the narrative. Or, in the case of neo-comedy, women are mere figures from magazines, neurotic prey for 'women's problems'.

We should ask ourselves what exactly is going on in cinema's impurification of the theatre actor. The reappearance within cinema of the subtle actor or actress – that is, one who would *divert* the evidence of the image through their acting, who would keep him or herself in reserve with regard to this evidence, and who would poetize it – such a reappearance would be welcome news, and it is news whose traces must be tracked down (they exist). Obviously what is in question in the film must allow the actor to act in such a way; this means that the gap between what is shown and the subjective fold of such showing must remain *measured*. Téchiné, for example, succeeds in doing just this in several sequences. In any case, what is certain is that one *cannot* lend support to a subtle actor if one incessantly juxtaposes him or her, as some sort of resistant *massivity*, to a visual and sonorous harassment, or, if his or her body and its gestures is abandoned to the interminable plasticity of neuroses.

7 A general hypothesis

At a completely global level, we can frame the particular enquiries which we have just set out by formulating, at our own risk, the following hypothesis: *The moment is one of neo-classicism.*

This hypothesis signifies three things:

– The strictly modern subtractive sequence (subtraction of the actor and of the narrative construction, prevalence of the text, indiscernibility of fiction and documentary, etc.) is saturated.

– No new configuration is perceptible *qua* event.
– What we see is an exasperated and overdrawn version of pre-existent schemas, or a manipulation to the second degree of these schemas, genres included, which are cited and submitted to a hystericization of their sources. This is what can be termed contemporary formalism. Its most general signature is the mobility of the camera which steps over the notion of the shot by aiming to join together, in a single movement, visible configurations which are disparate, or classically non-unifiable.

Yet, against formalism, whose encounter with any real is improbable, or exterior (hence the ends of formalist films, which most often relapse into sugared realism, as if saying or affirming supposed a renunciation of the movement of form) one can predict an academic reaction, which has even already begun here and there.

We will term neo-classical the effort at an internal purification of the academic reaction and its regime of visibility. There is already something of this genre in the best sequences of *The Titanic*, or even *Brassed Off*. It is a matter of operations which assume the reactive conjuncture, but which work it on the basis of the saturated modern sequence. A little like Picasso between the cubist sequence of the 1910s, and the opening, from the 1930s–40s onwards, of genuine non-figurative art. He accepted a certain return to representative forms, but he worked them from the standpoint of cubism itself.

Our last question will be: What are the few clues of such an effort worth today? What do they promise?

Notes

1 Translator's note: This article originally appeared as 'Considérations sur l'état actuel du cinéma', *L'Art du Cinéma* 24 (March 1999). The latter is a review appearing five times a year which collects the ongoing work of a number of researchers. See www.imaginet.fr/secav for their archives.
2 Translator's note: *L'Organisation politique* is the activist group of which Badiou is a founding member.
3 Translator's note: The PCF is the French Communist Party.

7

Philosophy and the 'death of communism'

Will the evocation of death allow us to find an appropriate way of naming what we have witnessed? Yet are we solely witnesses?[1] And besides, who is this 'we' that I am interrogating, and what could be said concerning *what* it is? There is no longer a 'we', there hasn't been for a long time. The 'we' entered into its twilight well before the 'death of communism'. Or rather, the dismantlement of the Soviet Party-State is nothing more than the objective crystallization (because objectivity, or representation, is always the State, or a state, a state of the situation) of the fact that a certain thought of 'we' has been inoperative for more than twenty years. For it was 'we communists', as a specification added to 'we revolutionaries', which in turn gave political and subjective force to the 'we' supposed as the ultimate referent, the 'we' of class, the 'we proletarians', that none declared, but that every ideal community posed prior to itself as a historical axiom. Or, in other words: We, faithful to the event of October '17.

When I say 'we communists', and even more so when I think of Lenin (it is of his thought that I think, and not of his precarious statues, even if nobody will ever make me say 'St Petersburg') or of the Russian revolution, I do not think of the party, a party that I have always fought, always held for what it has never ceased to be: the site of a politics which is both hesitant and brutal, the site of an arrogant incapacity. Even less so is it a matter of the USSR, despotic grey totality, reversal of October '17 into its contrary (politics under the condition of Lenin, the insurrection in its seizure and its catching hold, turned into the police-run blindness of the State). Thought's decisions and what they carry along with them at the level of more or less secret nominations are anterior to institutional figures. Presentation, multiplicity without concept, is never entirely grasped within representation. No, it was not a question of localizable entities, or apparatuses or symbols. There was something at stake, something which had the power of making us stand up in thought. For it is for thought in general that there was no other conceivable 'we' than that under the banner of communism. 'Communism' named the effective history of 'we'. It was in this manner that, as an adolescent, I understood Sartre's vulgar maxim: 'Every anti-communist is a dog,' for every anti-communist manifested his hatred of 'we', his determination to exist solely within the limits of *self*-possession – which is always the possession of a few goods.

Today the latent universal statement is that every communist is a dog. But this is not important – or rather no more important than the historical soiling of a noble word, which, after all, is the destiny of words, especially the most noble: to be dragged in blood and mud. It is not important, because the figure of 'we' to which this word was devoted has been long since abolished. The word no longer covered anything other than representation, the party, the State, the ineluctable usurpation, by the One's deadly lock down, of what was for a time the glorious uprise of the multiple. The 'Death of communism' signifies that, in the long term, what is dead in presentation – the emblematic 'we' under which, since October, or since 1793, political thought conditioned a philosophy of the community – must also die in representation. Whatever no longer has the force of the pure multiple can no longer preserve the powers of the One. We must rejoice in this: it is the mortality of the structural capacities of usurpation.

Of course, if required, at the level of the order of the State (of things) there is a 'death of communism'. But, for thought, it is no more than a second death. Outside the State, there among the emblem and the insurrection, 'communism' had, for a long time, named nothing more than the tomb of a secular 'we'.

That this death be a second death is attested by a remarkable fact of opinion, which is nevertheless real: the 'death of communism' is rhetorically deployed alongside the 'break up of the Soviet empire'. That 'communism' thus be tied to 'empire' in the destiny of what is mortal proves – since subjectively 'communism' named the universal community, the end of class, and thus the contrary of all empire – that this 'death' is only the event-of-dying of what is already dead.

'Event'? Does death come or arrive in the form of an event? And what is there to say of such a second or secondary death? I hold death to be a fact, an attestation of belonging subjacent to the neutral plasticity of natural being. Everything dies – which also means no death is an event. Death is found on the side of multiple being, of its ineluctable dissociation. Death is the return of the multiple to the void from which it is woven. Death is under the law of the multiple (or mathematical) essence of being *qua* being, it is indifferent to existence. '*Homo liber denulla re minus quam de morte cogitat,*' decidedly, Spinoza was right; there is nothing to be thought in death, even if it be the death of an empire, other than the intrinsic nullity of being.

Every event is an infinite proposition in the radical form of a singularity and a supplement. Everyone feels, and not without anxiety, that there is nothing proposed to us by the current dislocations. There was a Polish event, between the Gdansk strikes (or even earlier, during the formation of the KOR, the invention of an innovative *route* between workers and intellectuals) and Jaruzelski's coup d'état. There was the sketch of a German event, during the Leipzig protests. Even in Russia there was the uncertain attempt on the part of the Vorkouta miners. But of truth faithful to these irruptions, nothing, such that everything remains undecidable. Then Valesa, the Pope, Helmut Kohl, Yeltsin . . . Who would dare interpret these proper names in the burst or the lightning strike of an evental proposition? Who could cite one sole unheard-of statement, one sole nomination without precedent, in the erosion, both sudden and soft, undivided and confused, of the despotic form of the Party-State? These years will remain exemplary for the following: that an abrupt and complete transformation in a situation does not in any way signify that the grace of an event has occurred. I liked saying what we said before, to keep our distance from these 'movements' so celebrated by opinion: 'not everything which moves is red'.[2] In the serenity of the concept, let us say that not everything that changes is an event, and that surprise, speed, and disorder can be mere simulacra of the event, and not its promise of truth. The simulacra of the 'Romanian revolution', now recognized, also give us a paradigm. In truth, what has occurred is nothing more than this: what was subjectively dead must enter into the State of death, and finally be recognized there as such.

Moreover, how could the 'death of communism' be the name of an event once we remark that every historical event is communist, inasmuch as 'communist' designates the trans-temporal subjectivity of emancipation?

The *particular* figure constituted in the lineage of October '17 of 'we communists' has certainly been obsolete for a long time (since when? – a delicate question, which is not a matter of philosophy, but of politics. Politics alone, from the point of the prescription that opens it up, *thinks* the lacunary periodicity of political subjectivity.[3] In my eyes, in any case, it is at least since May '68 as far as France is concerned.) However, philosophically, 'communist' is not reducible to the finished sequence during which parties attributed the term to themselves, nor to the sequence during which the idea of a politics of emancipation was being debated under this name. For every word it seizes, however recent, philosophy seeks an in-temporal consonance. Philosophy exists solely insofar as it extracts concepts from a historical pressure which would grant them nothing other than a relative sense. What does 'communist' signify in an absolute sense? What is it that philosophy is able to think under this name (philosophy under the condition of a politics)? Egalitarian passion, the Idea of justice, the will to break with the compromises of the service of goods, the deposing of egotism, the intolerance of oppression, the vow of an end to the State;[4] the absolute pre-eminence of multiple-presentation over representation; the tenacious militant determination, set in motion by some incalculable event, to maintain, come what may, the proposition of a singularity without predicate, an infinity without determination or immanent hierarchy; what I term the generic, which – when its procedure is political – provides the ontological concept of democracy, or of communism, it's the same thing.[5]

This subjective *form*: philosophy recognizes that it has always been and will always be a constant escort of the great popular uprisings, when the latter are, precisely, not captive and opaque (as is everything shown to us today; nationalisms, the fascination of the market, mafiosi and demagogues, all hauled up high on the parliamentary mast), but in free rupture with being-in-situation, or counted-being, which would rein them in. From Spartacus to Mao (not the Mao of the State, who also exists, but the rebellious extreme, complicated Mao), from the Greek democratic insurrections to the worldwide decade 1966–76, it is and has been, in this sense, a question of communism. It will always be a question of communism, even if the word, soiled, is replaced by some other designation of the concept that it covers, the philosophical and thus eternal concept of rebellious subjectivity. I named such, around 1975, the 'communist invariants'.[6] I maintain the expression, against that of the 'death of communism'. And that – at the very moment in which a monstrous avatar, literally disastrous (a 'State of communism'!) is falling apart – it thus be a matter of the following: any event, which is politically foundational of truth, exposes the subject that it induces to the eternity of the equal. 'Communism', in having named this eternity, cannot adequately serve to name a death.

Here I shall strike up (before the prohibition of eternity prepared by any justification of commodities) a chant of which I am the author, a chant 'after the style of Saint-John Perse' as was said in the grand siècle, 'after the style of the Ancients'.[7] Written eighteen years ago, it was then in agreement with the leading active opinion, that of the revolutionaries of the period after May '68, and singularly of the Maoists. Published twelve years ago, it had already begun, again, to smack of heresy. Actually sung on stage seven years ago, it had become mysterious, strangely obstinate. And today?! As for myself, I have retouched it a little (certainly not in repentance of its sense, but simply because I have less of a taste for Saint-John Perse nowadays. Against aesthetic nihilism, I hold that convictions and commitment are more durable than tastes. *Must* be.) To these variations in its coincidence with the spirit of the times, the chant opposes a measure which is its own, and which touches upon, as we shall see, centuries, millennia. It is thus also (and this is why, even absolutely alone – which is not the case – I would murmur it here) a chant of announcement, the multiple name of what is always to come.

Who then spoke of solitude?
Defeated! Legendary defeated!
I call here for your unacceptance.
You: oppressed of backward times, slaves of the sun-sacrifice mutilated for the darkness of tombs. Men of great labour sold with the earth whose colour they bear. Children exiled by the closure of the fields to the service of cotton fabrics and coal.
For it is enough to wait, and to think: no one accepts, never.
Spartacus, Jacquou le croquant, Thomas Münzer.
You, vagabonds of the plain, Taïpings of the great loess, Chartists, Luddites, plotters from the labyrinth of the *faubourgs*, Babouvist

egalitarians, sans-culottes, communards, spartakists. All the people of popular sects and seditious parties, section-leaders of the time of the Terror, men of the pike and pitchfork, of the barricades and burnt castles.

The crowd of so many others: to have done with what they were; discovering in the declaration of their act the latent separating thought.

You: sailors throwing their officers to carnivorous fish, utopians of elegiac cities fighting in forest clearings, Quechua miners in the Andes greedy for dynamite. And these rebel Africans in successive tides amid the colonial stench under the protection of God and of shields of panthers. Without forgetting he who, all alone, took up his hunting rifle, as if for wild boars, and began the resistance to the aggressor in the forests of Europe.

For of what breaks the circle nothing is lost. No one forgets, ever.

Robespierre, Saint-Just, Blanqui, Varlin.

You: deployment in the streets of great processions of every kind. Sinister students, girls demanding the rights of women, banners of great clandestine trade unions, old-timers woken to the memory of general strikes, veterans of failed coups, workers on bikes.

The few-numbered (epochs against the grain): maintainers of the exact idea in the basements with hand-run presses. Thinkers of the obsolete and of the to-come. Sacrificial consciences white like the Rose. Or even those, armed with long bamboos who made a science out of the skewering of the fattest policemen, while all the rest remained obscure to them.

For, out of a dimensionless liberty, writing forms the innumerable.

Marx, Engels.

You: haranguers and warriors of the peasants' league, camisard prophets, women of clubs, of assemblies and federations, workers and high-school students from grassroots, action, triple union and grand alliance committees. Soviets of factories and military companies, popular tribunals, grand commissions of villagers for the redistribution of land, the filling of an irrigation dam, the formation of militia. Revolutionary groups for the control of prices, the execution of prevaricators and the surveillance of stocks.

For meditation upon what gathers and multiplies will not rest. Nothing is forever disseminated.

Lenin, Trotsky, Rosa Luxembourg, Chou en Laï, Mao Tse-tung.

All of you. You judge what is lacking and you examine the abolition: 'Who speaks of failure? What was done and thought was done and thought. In its beginning, its time and its caesura. Leave the weighing of results to the accountants. For what was at stake in our reign was the invention of separation, and not the establishment of the weighty office of a duration.
The infinity of situations, who then will exhaust them? The event in which the dice are cast, who then will appease it?
Trust yourself to your imperative. Turn yourself away from power. That you be indifferent to the verdict, and that nothing in you ever consents.
To necessity.
The satisfied, they can pass on. The fearful, they can proliferate. It is our intact singularity which has made this great hole in the world in which, century after century, the semaphore of communism is fixed.'

The glancing light of the semaphore, the illumination of centuries by the rare pivoting insurrection of this light; would this all be extinct because a mediocre tyranny decided to take it upon itself to announce that it was dead? This is exactly what I do not believe.

Note that it is not the uprisen solar masses who decided the end of the Party-State, the end of the Soviet empire. The regulating of this elephant occurred through an internal disordering, which was both concerted and yet devoid of perspective. The affair to this day has remained entirely a state affair. No political invention – or invention of politics – has lent any articulation to the circumstance.[8] That thousands of people marked here or there, in the streets and in a few factories, that they were happy with what was happening was the least that they could do! But an indication that they thought and wanted the experience of a novelty without precedent, alas, that was not observed. And how could it have been otherwise if it is true, as affirmed by all and sundry, that what they think and want, the people of Russia and Hungary and Bulgaria, is nothing other than what already exists, and has done for quite a while, in our sad countries called, who knows why, 'Western'? Such a will can do nothing but comfort the pre-eminence of the state and constitutional views of these processes. Elections and property owners, politicians and racketeers: is this all they want? If so, it is quite reasonable to trust the execution of such processes, not to the inventions of thought, but to specialists in the manoeuvre of apparatuses, indeed to the experts of the

International Monetary Fund. As for a little supplement for the soul, the Pope is in on the affair. And as for a touch of passionate excess – without which the simulacrum of an event would be far too peaceful – there will be a search among history as far back as before the war of 1914 to find the means to cast one bestial nationality against another.

If there is no event, it is because what is at stake is the history of States, and in no way the history of politics. This distinction is crucial. It is easy to object that the history of communism tied the 'Soviet' state paradigm to militant subjectivity, and that the dismantling of one closed down the other. I maintain the opposite thesis: militant subjectivity, philosophically received in the form of the 'we', was obsolete or inactive well before the system of the Party-State entered into the sequence of its ruin.

What exact role did the 'Soviet paradise' play in the subjective, that is political, constitution of militancy named communist? It is a major theme of received opinion that it played an important role, and that the 'revelations' – for example, those of Solzhenitsyn – of state and Stalinist infamy bore a fatal blow to 'utopia'. But this story does not stand up, just like any story which tries to describe a subjectivity (in this case, political) under the categories of lies, error and illusion. No *real* political figure organizes its consistency around the nothingness of a fallacious representation, nor has a paradigm (a State or a norm) at the centre of its determinations. Certainly, October '17 as event engages practical fidelities, but the thought which cements them together depends on the event as such, and not on its state projection. And the becoming of these fidelities is tributary, not to propaganda (servile vision of consciousnesses), but to situations. The force of the communist reference in France owes its fate (debatable, but from an entirely different point of view) first of all to the outcome of the First World War, then to the Popular Front, then to antifascism and the Resistance; and very little to the anarchic and bloody history of the Soviet State. Any systematic conjunction with the history of that State has bought itself, not an increase in power, but painful weakness and difficult crises. In the same manner, in order to create his own resource in historicity, Mao thinks not the Russian economy but the Chinese peasantry and the struggle against the Japanese invasion. At the level of subjectivity, the concrete history of communisms (I refer to them this time in their common identity, that of parties, groups, militants, official or dissident) does not rely upon the 'paradisaical' State, which serves solely as a random objectification. At the beginning, the most inventive, those who attuned the party to the essential history of the place in which its actions took place, Mao, Tito, Enver Hoxha; all of them finished by breaking with the matrix of the Soviet State – they saw clearly that its objectivity did not even serve their immediate intentions.

How, otherwise, can one explain that this sequential communism reached its greatest power, including its seduction for thought, between 1930 and 1960; that is, in the very epoch in which the Stalinist crimes were unleashed? And that it entered into its twilight from Brezhnev onwards, an era of 'stagnation' in which people were no longer killed, and in which the physiognomy of the State, always a little repugnant, nevertheless bore comparison to that of, let's say, the United States of the Vietnam War, or to that of the Brazil of the security guerillas (where, apparently, a superb market economy reigns)? What explanation is there? The blindness of faith? But why faith when everything is getting worse, and the weakening of such faith when everything is not as bad? Ignorance, that useful contingency?

There is a hypothesis which is both stronger and simpler: it is that the political and thus subjective history of communisms is essentially divided from their State history. The criminal objectivity of the Stalinist State is one thing, the militant subjectivity of communists is another; the latter has its own referents, its own singular development, and its own non-objective prescriptions. Criminal objectivity only ever functioned as a *general* argument – it has always perfectly functioned for reactionaries, read *Tintin in the land of the Soviets*, a 1929 text – inasmuch as political subjectivity, the sequential 'we', was obsolete.

It is not the revelation of crime, by Solzhenitsyn or anyone else, which ruined the political hypothesis of communism ('communism' understood here within the twentieth century's sequence of 'we'). It is the death – once again, the ancient death – of the hypothesis which allowed these 'revelations' to have such efficacy. Because if political subjectivity has become unable to support, by itself, in thought and in act, the singularity of its trajectory (and thus also its philosophical connection to emancipatory eternity, to the invariants), then there is no longer any other reference than that of the State, and it is true that the criminal character of such and such State becomes an argument without answer.

It is not because the Stalinist state was criminal that the Leninist prescriptions, crystallized in October '17, ceased to expose communism to its eternity within time (moreover, what relation is there between these prescriptions, that event and the Stalinist State, apart from pure empirical consequence?). It is because there were no longer any possible militants of such an exposition, for intrinsic and purely political reasons, that the Stalinist State – once it had *retroactively* become the absurd incarnation of the Idea – functioned as an unanswerable historical argument against the Idea itself.

This is why the ruin of the Party-State is a process immanent to *the history of States*. It succumbs to its objective solitude, to its subjective abandon. It succumbs by the absenting of politics, and singularly of any politics deserving the name 'communist'. The anarchic confused deplorable spectacle – but necessary and legitimate because what is dead must die – of this ruin testifies, not to the 'death of communism', but to the immense consequences *of its lack*.

Notes

1   Translator's note: The original text formed the first chapter of A. Badiou, *D'un désastre obscur* (Paris: Editions de l'aube, 1998), 7–25.
2   Translator's note: In French the slogan rhymes: 'Tout ce qui bouge n'est pas rouge.'
3   The philosophical statement about these questions is limited to posing the rarity of politics as generic procedure, its discontinuous existence. In my *Théorie du sujet* (Paris: Seuil, 1982) I formulate this in the following terms: 'Every subject is political. This is why there are few subjects, and little politics.' The body of philosophical statements concerning this point is very complex. It involves the doctrine, founded by Sylvain Lazarus, of *historical modes of politics*.
4   Translator's note: The service of goods (*le service des biens*) is a phrase coined by Lacan to designate political and social organization functioning under the register of demand, rather than that of desire. See J. Lacan, *Seminar VII: The Ethics of Psychoanalysis 1959–60*, trans. D. Porter (London: Routledge, 1992).
5   The generic – that is, the status in thought of the infinite multiplicity as *any multiplicity whatsoever*, as the materiality of a truth – is the most important concept advanced by the philosophical propositions of my book *L'Etre et l'événement* (Paris: Seuil, 1988) [*Being and Event*, trans. O. Feltham (London: Continuum Books, forthcoming)].
6   The theory of communist invariants is sketched in my little book, written in collaboration with François Balmès, *De l'idéologie* (Paris: Maspéro, 1976).
7   This 'chorus of the divisible defeat' is an extract from *L'Echarpe rouge*, romanopéra (Paris: Maspéro, 1976). Reworked, the 'romanopéra' became the libretto of a real opera, for which Georges Aperghis composed the music, and which was performed at the Lyon opera, at Avignon, then at Chaillot, in a staging by Antoine Vitez with sets by Yannis Kokkos in 1984. The chorus,

over astonishing, complex and violent music, was sung by all of the opera's players, in emblematic workers' outfits. Pierre Vial crossed the stage, sheltering from who knows what storm via the effect of an old umbrella. He had the air of a survivor, of a tramp of eternal insurrections, and he grumbled 'communism! communism!' in an unforgettable manner.

Once again, the unappeasable pain caused in me by the death of Antoine Vitez. The 'death of communism', how it tormented him! And yet, how he managed to hold onto it with his clarity! His text 'Ce qui nous reste' ['What remains for us'] must be read, from 1990, so close to his death. It is included in the precious and loyal collection proposed by Danièle Sallenave and Georges Banu, under the title *Le théâtre des idées* (Paris: Gallimard, 1991). I would like to cite the eighth statement from this text: 'The crime – what can be termed for simplification Stalin's crime, but it clearly goes beyond Stalin – is that of leaving hope in the hands of the irrational, of obscurantists, of demagogues.' But after the execution of the crime, Antoine Vitez, as always, goes straight to prescriptions. To what he calls 'our role': 'sarcasm, invective and prediction, critique of the current times, announce'. In these few pages I am, I think, a player of this 'role'. There will be many others.

8 'The invention of politics' is the title of a book – the last – by Moses Finley, the great historian of antiquity. It is a significant reference in the theoretical work of Sylvain Lazarus. His commentary can be read in S. Lazarus, *L'Anthropologie du nom* (Paris: Seuil, 1996).

8

Philosophy and the 'war against terrorism'

A Method

Faced with the destruction of New York's Twin Towers by planes whose passengers, like the neo-pilots – those assassinating impostors – were transformed into incendiary projectiles, there was, everywhere, the evidence of a certain affect.[1] For those who more or less secretly celebrated – an extremely numerous crowd, hundreds of millions of human beings, all enemies of the lugubrious and solitary American superpower – it was nevertheless a matter of an unbelievable mass crime. 'Attack' is an inappropriate word; it evokes the nihilist bombings of the Tsar's coaches, or the attack of Sarajevo – it has a *fin de siècle* resonance to it, but that of another century. At the beginning of this millennium, the evidence of that affect registers the extraordinary combination of violence, calm, quiet relentlessness, organization, indifference to fire, agony and destruction, which was necessary in conditions of such technological sophistication to bring about the death of many thousands of common people and ordinary workers deep in the heart of a great metropolis. It was an enormous murder, lengthily premeditated, and yet silent. No one has claimed responsibility for it. That is why one could say that, formally speaking, this mass crime – which aimed, anonymously and with the most perfect cruelty, to destabilize a 'normal' situation – conjures up the fascist concept of action. And as a consequence, everywhere throughout the world, and quite apart from the immediate position of one's soul – devastated or complicit – there was a paralysing stupefaction, a kind of paroxysmally denied disbelief: the affect that signals a disaster.

Philosophy, of course, must take the *evidence* of this affect into account. Nevertheless it is also philosophy's duty to not remain satisfied with affect. Religion may declare its trust in the heart's self-evidences. Art, says Gilles Deleuze, gives form to percepts and affects. Philosophy, however, must depart from the latter to arrive at the concept – this is its arid destination – no matter how traumatic the point from which its research departs, or a construction is undertaken.

As such, a second kind of evidence is proposed to philosophical labour; this time not that of an affect, but of a name, the name 'terrorism'. This nominal evidence (that the mass crime of New York – signalled by the affect of the disaster – is a terrorist action) has since played a decisive role. By fixing a designated enemy, it has cemented a world coalition, authorized the UN to declare that the US is in a state of 'legitimate defence', and initiated the programming of the targets of vengeance. At a deeper level, the word 'terrorism' has a triple function:

1. It determines a subject – this is the subject who is targeted by the terrorist act, who is struck, who is plunged into mourning and who must lead the vengeful riposte. This subject is named either 'Our Societies', or 'The West', or 'The Democracies' or, even, 'America' – but the latter at the price, swiftly paid by the editors, that 'we' are 'all American'.
2. It supports predicates – on this occasion terrorism is 'Islamic'.
3. It determines a sequence – the entire current sequence is from now on considered as 'the war against terrorism'. We are warned that it will be a long war, an entire epoch. In short, the 'war against Islamic terrorism' takes over from the Cold (and Hot: Korea, Vietnam, Cuba ...) War against communism.

There, once again, philosophy has a duty: if it is to register the widespread evidence of the word 'terrorism' as an important symptom, then it must examine the latter's origin and application.

In short, there are two rules to the method. First, philosophy is never transitive to affect no matter how widespread the latter might be. A crime is a crime, agreed. But the consequences of a crime – even one that, formally, is fascistic – cannot mechanically be other crimes. And this designation, 'crime', should also be applied to State crimes, including those – innumerable – committed by 'democratic' States. As we well know – in fact, at the least since Aeschylus' *Oresteia* and thus for a long time – the question is always to know how to reinstate justice in the place of vengeance.

Second, however commonly held the dominant nominations may be, philosophy cannot accept them without critical examination. Philosophy knows that in general such nominations are under the control of the powers that be and their propaganda.

As such, we will proceed to a meticulous examination of names. Our point of departure will be the central name, 'terrorism'. Then, following upon that, we will submit the trio of the predicate ('Islamic'), the subject ('The West'), and the sequence ('the war against terrorism') to critique.

B Terrorism?

Originally, a 'terrorist' was someone who legitimated and practised Terror. It was an objective designation that was only defamatory for certain political adversaries. For example, during the French Revolution the Grand Jacobins of the Committee for Public Safety had no problem declaring themselves 'terrorists'. They officially made Terror part of daily business. By that they meant a provisional but complete confusion of political and judicial power, justified by exceptional circumstances (civil war and war), the repressive deployment of expeditious measures without appeal, and widespread recourse to the death penalty. Terror was explicitly thought of as a contingent necessity (Robespierre was known for his categorical and principled opposition to the death penalty) when political virtue – that is, the republican conviction – was still too precarious to assure victory over the enormous coalition of domestic and foreign counter-revolutionaries. Saint-Just asked – 'What do they want, those who want neither terror nor virtue?' The Thermidorians provided the response – they wanted the end of the revolution, the reign of corruption, and suffrage for the wealthy alone.

It is remarkable that the word 'terrorism', which clearly qualified a particular figure of the exercise of State power, has come, little by little, to signify exactly the contrary. Indeed, for a long time now the word 'terrorist' has been used by the State to designate all violent and/or armed political adversaries, precisely in view of their non-State character. As examples we can list the Russian terrorists of *Narodnaia Volia* at the end of the last century; all those of the anarchist tradition, including the *Bande à Bonnot* in France; and the character of Chen, in *Man's Fate*, who, already, incarnated the decision of the suicide attack and to which Malraux gave –

without justifying it politically – a terrible grandeur. But the word has finally come to designate – and it is here that it takes on a negative connotation – from the position of the dominant, all those who engage in a combat, using whatever means at hand, against a given order which is judged to be unacceptable. 'Terrorists', the anti-Nazi resistors for Pétain and his militia; 'terrorists', the Algerian patriots of the NLF for every French government without exception between 1954 and 1962; as are also the Palestinian fighters for the State of Israel, and the Chechens for Putin and his clique. 'Terrorists' lastly, for Bush and his servile patriotic opinion, the nebulous, or at least extremely opaque, group of those who attack and incriminate Americans' goods and lives.

It must be said that today, at the end of its semantic evolution, the word 'terrorist' is an intrinsically propagandistic term. It has no neutral readability. It dispenses with all reasoned examination of political situations, of their causes and consequences.

In fact, it is a term that has become essentially formal. 'Terrorist' no longer designates a political orientation or the possibilities of such and such a situation, but rather, and exclusively, the form of action. And it does so according to three criteria. It is first and foremost – for public opinion and those who attempt to shape it – a spectacular, non-State action, which emerges – reality or myth – from clandestine networks. Second, it is a violent action aiming to kill or destroy. Lastly, it is an action which makes no distinction between civilians and non-civilians.

This formalism approaches Kant's moral formalism. This is why a 'moral philosophy' specialist like Monique Canto believed she could declare that the absolute condemnation of 'terrorist' actions and the symmetrical approval of reprisals, including those of Sharon in Palestine, could and should precede any examination of the situation, and be abstracted from any concrete political considerations. When it is a matter of 'terrorism', according to this Iron lady of a new breed, to explain is already to justify. It is thus appropriate to punish without delay and without further examination. Henceforth, 'terrorism' qualifies an action as the formal figure of Evil. Moreover, this is exactly how Bush from the very beginning conceived of the deployment of vengeance: Good (in concrete, State terrorism directed against peasant villages and the ancient cities of Central Asia) against Evil (non-State terrorism directed at 'Western' buildings).

It is at this point, where rationality risks collapsing beneath the immensity of the propagandistic evidence, that one must be careful with the details. In particular, one must examine the effects of the nominal chain induced by the passage from the adjective 'terrorist' – as the formal qualification of an action – to the substantive 'terrorism'. Indeed, such is the moment when, insidiously, form becomes substance. Three kinds of effect are thereby rendered possible: a subject-effect (facing 'terrorism' is a 'we' avenging itself); an alterity-effect (this 'terrorism' is the other of Civilization, the 'Islamic' barbarian); and finally, a periodization-effect (now commences the long 'war against terrorism').

C Who is this 'we' facing terrorism?

It is obvious that 'terrorism' is a non-existent substance, an empty name. But this void is precious because it can be filled. And, first of all, as always, it is filled (as it was for 'the Boche' or 'the Jew') by that which is supposed to be opposed to it (the 'Frenchman' or the 'Aryan'). On this occasion, facing 'terrorism' there is a 'we' defending itself. Now, outside America – a name sufficient for American imperialist patriotism but hardly so for the anti-terrorist coalition, except if 'we are all American', which even the committed anti-terrorists balk at declaring – three names have been found for this 'we' facing the beast: a perilous but weighty name, 'the West'; a neutral name, 'our societies'; and a legitimating name, 'the democracies'.

In relation to the first of these names, it is regrettable to have to note that philosophy compromised itself there long ago; what with *The Decline of the West* – Spengler's best-seller – at the end of the nineteenth century, and with what continues nowadays in the phrase 'the end of Western metaphysics'. The 'Western' appropriation of thought – which is nothing but the intellectual trace of four centuries of imperialism – resounds right up to and including the opposition of the West (Christian? Jewish?) to 'Islamic terrorism'. Apart from anything else, let us recall for the younger generations that for decades the political use of the term 'the Occident' was confined to the racist extreme right, to the point of being the name of one of its most violent groupuscules.[2] Moreover, it seems to us that the litany of colonial atrocities committed throughout the entire world, the savagery of the world-scale slaughters, the wars of national liberation in Asia, the Middle-East and Africa, the armed revolts in Latin America, the universal value of the Chinese revolution, and the febrile sterility of the world in which we live, is sufficient for those who see an opposition being drawn up between 'Western values' and 'Terrorism' to conclude that 'terrorism' is a hollow word.

When 'our societies' are spoken of and it is declared that 'terrorism' wanted to 'strike them in their very heart' or 'destabilize' them, let us agree that what is being referred to is either still 'the West' but in a more demure fashion, or it is a material paradigm; a certain state of objective wealth which, in itself, has no kind of value for the philosopher and furthermore which would not be able to ground any kind of consistent solidarity. If this is not the case, then why does the crime of New York affect 'our societies', while neither the millions of AIDS deaths in Africa nor the genocidal disasters in Rwanda affect them in any way? 'Our societies', designating in a faintly obscene manner the completely relative well-being of some of the wealthiest human groups (minorities) on the planet, hardly make for a presentable face-off against the supposed substance of terrorism. Even if Monique Canto – her again – judges that it is philosophically superior and indispensable in the situation to remind us that being very rich is not a moral fault. Yet, to go against the grain of her formalist zeal, we would only grant her such a point after a meticulous and concrete examination of the origins of the wealth in question. For it could well be that all genuinely considerable wealth today is entirely, and by way of necessity, implicated in certain indubitable crimes.

Of the three names for 'us' only the third, fundamentally propagandistic, remains: what 'terrorism' targets is the 'Democracies', and in their heart, that exemplary democracy which we all know as the United States of America. As any old patriot from over there will tell you, 'it's a free country', and those Saudi fanatics, that's what they wanted to mutilate. 'Terrorism against democracy'; such is the formula for *consensus*. I mean, for the overwhelming majority of our contemporaries: here, in this jaded 'democratic' country, France, the sole space for a political inscription of the mass crime of New York is the one outlined by that formula. It is this formula which has neutralized reactions and generated general support, albeit a little plaintive, for the American war. Finally, it has been conceded that, in any case, if the democracies are attacked by terrorism then, in view of their excellence, they have the right to avenge themselves. What remains to be known is against whom these legitimate reprisals are to be carried out.

D 'Terrorism': substance and predicates

At this point let us introduce a precise philosophical proposition: every substantialization of a formal adjective requires a dominant predicate. If one goes from the adjective 'terrorist', which qualifies an action by its form, to 'terrorism', which is an empty substantive, one cannot hope to 'fill' such a void by its adversary alone (The West, Democracy, etc.). It is also necessary to endow it with a predicate (just as it was necessary around 1914, for all intents and purposes, that the Boche be bestial and – contrary to the reflective and Cartesian Frenchman – delivered over to obscure and instinctive forces, while around 1933 the Jew had to be cosmopolitan and abstract – contrary to the Aryan, tied to blood and soil. Today, the supposed substantial support called 'terrorism' only has being inasmuch as it receives the predicate 'Islamic'.

What exactly is the value of this predicate? One might be satisfied by saying that it has already been corrupted by its function, which is to furnish this 'Terrorism' with a semblance of historical colour. Taken on its own it comes down to the observation that religion has been subjected to political instrumentalization; another ancient 'Western' story, the wily alliances between the State and the Church do not date from yesterday. In any case, the conjunction of religion and all kinds of political processes, some extremely violent, is not a particularity of Islam. Think of religion – Catholicism in Poland for example – and the important role it played in the resistance against communism; whenever that occurred religion was congratulated by the 'democratic' states.

In the case at hand, that of Bin Laden – if, however, it really concerns him, which nobody up to this date has been able to prove – what is certain is that the point of departure is a series of extraordinary complex manoeuvres in relation to the manna of oilfields in Saudi Arabia and that the character is, after all, a good American: someone for whom what matters is wealth and power, and for whom the means are of less concern. Such are his rivals also, his comrades in power in the region. As far as making terror reign in the name of pure hard-line Islamic fundamentalism, the sovereigns of Saudi Arabia know what they're doing, yet to my knowledge not a single notable democrat has ever asked for an armada of B-52s to go and wipe them out. It must be strongly suspected, then, that for these democrats there is both 'Islamic terrorism' *and* 'islamic Terrorism'. The first, supported by the Americans and by way of consequence a friend to 'our societies', is to be, if not admired, then at least tolerated: turn a blind eye and keep going. The second, which managed to strike 'us' by means of its devious calculations: stigmatize it and bomb it into annihilation! In the final analysis, it is a matter of knowing how one is situated with regard to access to oil.

In passing, let us underline Wagner's prophetic virtue when, in his trilogy, he staged the curse attached to the Rhine's gold. Indeed, it is one of the great modern curses to have the equivalent of that gold in one's subsoil. South Africa's diamonds, Bolivia's tin-metal, the precious stones of the Congo and Sierra Leone, the oil in the Middle East and the Congo – as many regions or countries put to fire and the sword, become the stakes of rapacious and cynical calculations, because the planetary administration of their mineral resources necessarily escapes them. Let us note in passing that it does not seem as if 'Our Societies', our paradigmatic 'Democracies', as for what concerns them, draw the least consequence from these atrocious disasters. In any case, if like the god Wotan Bin Laden speaks at length, and somewhat confusedly, of destiny and religion, it seems that his business is rather that of knowing how to seize some black gold such as to inherit that Nibelungen collection, the Gulf petroleum monarchies.

It is worth remarking that the political instrumentalization of religion has in turn been persistently instrumentalized by the United States themselves. This has been one of the great constants of their politics for decades. Fearing Soviet influence, they fought everything that even mildly resembled secular politics in the Arab world. Whether Nasser in Egypt, or de Baas in Iraq, or in Syria, the United States did not get involved except to create more and more serious problems for these leaders, while on the other hand they supported without fail the retrograde fanatics of Saudi Arabia, Kuwait and Pakistan. In Indonesia they lent a helping hand to the eradication of a progressive pro-third-world regime by encouraging a Saint Bartholomew of communists, or of alleged communists, bringing about the death of five thousand. In Palestine everyone knows that from the very beginning the Israeli services considered the development of Hamas to be an excellent thing; against the Fatah hegemony, whose slogan, as you may recall, was for a secular democratic Palestine, and which included a number of Christians in its ranks. Finally, the Talibani themselves are a joint creature of the Americans and the Pakistanis, set in place against any takeover of power in Kabul by groups which were potential allies of either the Russians, the Chinese, or the Iranians. Taken in their entirety these manoeuvres disqualify the relevance of the predicate 'Islamic' when it is a matter of designating the 'terrorist' enemies of the United States.

Let us note the singular status of what we can call the instrumentalization of an instrumentalization. In the Middle East or elsewhere, certain cliques of politicians instrumentalize religion in order to facilitate their projects (in fact: in order to take over power from other ageing or discredited cliques of politicians). American governments regularly attempt to instrumentalize that instrumentalization, with a view to maintaining control over this or that situation. But the instrumentalization of an instrumentalization is a delicate mechanism. It is exposed to brutal deviations. In this manner, the United States (and the French who were very active at the time) instrumentalized Saddam Hussein, who instrumentalized the opposition between the Sunnites and the Shiites against his Iranian neighbours. The goal of the 'Western' powers was to derail the Iranian revolution, while Saddam Hussein's goal was to set himself up as a great regional power. The result: a terrifying war on the scale of the war of 1914–18, hundreds of thousands dead, the consolidation of the Iranian regime, and Saddam Hussein becoming an uncontrollable creature, then a 'terrorist' enemy. Inasmuch as the same story has reoccurred with the Talibani, we propose to all States the following maxim: 'Be extremely careful when instrumentalizing an instrumentalization,' especially one including religion, a subjective sustenance that does not let itself be easily manipulated by cruel and underhand politicians.

What the predicate 'Islamic' actually does is dissimulate a number of unappetizing (state) political operations, that are important to keep from public attention, *behind* 'cultural' categories whose subjective resources can be quite easily activated. In France, it is very easy to awaken an anti-Arab zeal for a thousand reasons, whether in the vulgar and post-colonialist form given to it by the extreme right, or in the more historical and 'ethical' form given to it by the Zionist or feminist intellectual petit-bourgeoisie. Thus we will see some rejoicing that Kabul is being bombarded to 'liberate Afghani women', others saying to themselves that Israel can always procure some benefits from the situation, while a third lot will think that a massacre of 'Bougnouls'[3] is always a good thing. None of all this has anything to do with the crime of New York, neither in the latter's causes, nor in its form, nor in its real effects. But all of them, validating the syntagm 'Islamic terrorism', rally behind the flag of the vengeful crusade, a crusade of various enthusiasms, and especially of innumerable apathies.

The philosophical lesson is thus the following: when a predicate is attributed to a *formal* substance (as is the case with any derivation of a substantive from a formal adjective) it has no other consistency than that of giving an ostensible content to that form. In 'Islamic terrorism', the predicate 'Islamic' has no other function except that of supplying an apparent content to the word 'terrorism' which is itself devoid of all content (in this instance, political). What is at stake is an artificial historicization which leaves what really happened (the crime of New York) unthought. This does not prohibit, but rather commands that what originates in that unthought – in the name of the inconsistent term designating it ('Islamic terrorism') – be a sort of *trompe l'oeil* history of the period which has just opened.

E   What 'war' against terrorism?

What is coming, our leaders tell us, is the 'war of the democracies against Islamic terrorism'; a long and difficult period.

But why a 'war'? Just as with 'terrorism' and 'Islamic' this word is extremely problematic in relation to the situation. What we will maintain here is that 'war' is the symmetrical term – it is also entirely formal – to the very vague 'terrorism'.

It is important to register that the usage of the term 'war' (immediately employed by high American officials in their declarations, and then by their governmental and opinion-making servants) is something new. Previously, when governments declared that their duty was 'to eradicate terrorism', they were careful not to speak of war. Indeed, how does one declare war upon a few delinquent civilians or a bunch of fanatical bombers or upon a group of anarchists? The word 'war' is far too dignified; moreover, it has been assigned far too exclusively to conflicts between states for such usage. Even during the endless and very violent colonial war against the Algerian patriots, which mobilized hundreds of thousands of soldiers, French governments from Mitterand to De Gaulle always spoke of 'maintaining order' and of 'pacification'. Even today, using the same methods as the French in Algeria forty years ago in order to settle accounts with Chechen nationalists (systematic torture, internment camps, destruction of villages, rape) Putin carefully avoids saying that there is, strictly speaking, a war. It is an immense police operation, wherein, to employ his own expression, 'we will go looking for the terrorists right into the sewers' and so on. In sum, governments have opposed repression to terrorism, generally using the most violent and abject of means, but always within the symbolic register of policing.

Why then, in the case that concerns us here, is it a matter of war, including, or even especially, at the level of the symbolic register? The crime of New York, like all crime, calls for police mobilization in order to track down and judge its authors or its financial backers. Without doubt, in doing so, the modern 'services' will use fear and extremely unethical methods. But war?

My thesis is that the American imperial power, in the formal representation it makes of itself, has war as the privileged, indeed unique, form of the attestation of its existence. Moreover, one can observe today that the powerful subjective unity that carries the Americans away in their desire for vengeance and war is immediately constructed around the flag and the army.

The United States has become a hegemonic power in and through war: from the civil war, said to be that of Secession (the first modern war due to its industrial means and the number of deaths); then the two World Wars; and finally the uninterrupted series of local wars and military interventions of all kinds since the Korean War up until the present ransacking of Afghanistan, passing via Lebanon, the Bay of Pigs, Vietnam, Libya, Panama, Barbados, the Gulf War, and Serbia, not to mention their persistent support for Israel in its endless war against the Palestinians. Of course, one will hasten to add that the USA won the day in the Cold War against the USSR on the terrain of military rivalry (Reagan's Star Wars project pushed the Russians to throw in the towel) and intend to do the same thing against China, hoping to discourage any project of great magnitude by the imposition of an exhausting armament race (this is the only sense possessed by the pharaonic anti-missile shield project).

This should remind us, in these times of economic obsession, that power continues to be, in the last instance, military. Even the USSR, however run-down it was, inasmuch as it was considered as an important military power (and above all by the Americans), it continued to co-direct the world. Today the USA has the monopoly over aggressive protection via enormous forces of destruction, and it does not hesitate to use them. The consequences are evident, including (notably) the idea that the American people has of itself and of what must be done. Let us hope that the Europeans – and the Chinese – draw the obvious lesson from the situation: those who do not watch carefully over their armed forces are promised nothing, save servitude.

Being forged in this fashion amid the continual barbarity of war – leaving aside the genocide of the Indians and the importation of tens of millions of black slaves – the USA quite naturally considers that the only riposte worthy of them is a spectacular staging of power. The particular adversary chosen matters very little, in fact, and can be entirely disconnected from the initial crime. The pure capacity to destroy this or that will do the job, even if the latter ends up being a few thousand poor devils or a phantom 'government'. In the end, any war is suitable, as long as the appearance of victory is overwhelming.

What we have here (and will also have if the USA continues in Somalia and in Iraq, etc.) is war as the abstract form of a theatrical capture of an adversary ('terrorism') which in its essence is vague and elusive. The war against nothing: save against what is itself removed from any war.

F   Parenthesis on 'anti-Americanism'

Certain 'intellectuals' have judged the moment ripe to stigmatize the compulsive anti-Americanism to which French intellectuals are occasional victims. It is well known that in this type of polemic, those whom the journalist-intellectuals call 'French intellectuals' are the other journalist-intellectuals who don't share their position. As a result, the more the word 'intellectual' is emphasized the more intellectuality itself is absent. It is a requirement of this debate that each camp declares itself to be persecuted and in the minority, at least insofar as it is composed solely of veterans who can be seen every day on television, and whose countenance or loquaciousness one cannot help but admire if one picks up a magazine. We have thus been treated to the spectacle of Jacques Juillard and Bernard-Henri Lévy, two particularly copious editorialists, presenting themselves as the solitary dispensers of justice, worn down by dint of their good fight for liberty and modernity against the enslaving, archaic, and repulsive horde of French intellectuals.

The central argument of these heroes of the fraternal alliance with the American bombers amounts to the following: that to be against the USA in this affair, as in many others, is to be against freedom. It is as simple as that. Bernard Henri-Lévy, who is never particular about details, states that anti-Americanism is fascistic. As for Julliard – literally in his own twilight by dint of having been right all along – his axiom is that 'French intellectuals' do not like freedom.

We could be satisfied in saying that an orientation of thought, for the sole reason that Bernard-Henri Lévy has declared it fascist, at the very least deserves to be considered with attention. We would hasten to add that if 'freedom' is that of politically and intellectually resembling Jacques Juillard, then it is assuredly better not to be free.

But what we will say is this: if there exists one unique great imperial power which is always convinced that its most brutal interests coincide with the Good; if it is true that every year the USA spends more on their military budget than Russia, China, France, England and Germany put together; and if that Nation-State, devoted to military excess, has no public idol other than wealth, no allies other than servants, and no view of other peoples apart from an indifferent, commercial, and cynical one; then the basic freedom of States, peoples and individuals consists in doing everything and thinking everything in order to escape, as much as possible, from the commandments, interventions and interference of that imperial power.

'Anti-Americanism' is meaningless. The American people have brought humanity admirable inventions in all orders of experience. But today there cannot be the least political liberty or independence of mind, without a constant and unrelenting struggle against the *imperium* of the USA.

One can, of course, have as one's sole ambition to be considered by the masters in Washington as their most zealous servant. It seems sometimes as if Tony Blair dreams of a posthumous repose for his Old England; that of becoming the 51st state of the Union. He is reminiscent of those vassal 'Kings' of Rome, whose pusillanimity is depicted in certain of Corneille's tragedies: 'Ah! Don't put me on bad terms with the [Roman] Republic!' says Prusias, Bithynie's Pétain, to Nicomede, the potential resistance fighter. Let's take the liberty of siding with Nicomede and considering that the inevitable condition of our freedom is that of being at odds, seriously at odds, with American 'democracy', just like Corneille's hero with the Roman 'Republic'. At odds, one might say, 'till death'. For the American superpower is nothing but the deadly guarantee of the obscene accumulation of wealth. The American army is the instrument of the Race of 'Western' lords against the wretched of the entire planet.

G   The disjunctive synthesis of two nihilisms

We can now return to our point of departure: philosophy facing the event. We have reached the important critical stage which is that of the destitution of terms. Of the consensual statement 'the war of the Democracies against Islamic Terrorism' more or less nothing intelligible remains.

What, then, is our own formula? Joyfully borrowing a concept from Gilles Deleuze we shall say: What is testified to by the crime of New York and the following battles is the *disjunctive synthesis of two nihilisms*.

Let's clarify this aphorism.

There is a synthesis, because, to our mind, the principal actors in this matter belong to the same species. Yes, Bin Laden, or whoever financed the crime, despite being on one side, and the foundations of the American superpower on the other; these two belong to the same world, that – nihilistic – of money, of blind power, of cynical rivalry, of the hidden gold of primary resources, of total scorn for peoples' everyday lives, and of the arrogance of a self-certitude based on the void. And moral and religious platitudes plated onto all that: on both sides Good, Evil, and God serve as rhetorical ornaments to jousts of financial ferocity and to schemes for hegemonic power.

There is a disjunction in that it is inevitably through the form of crime that these actors seek and find each other. Whether the crime is the private, secretly machinated and suicidal crime of New York, or whether it is that of Kabul, Kandahar, and elsewhere – a State crime reinforced with anaesthetized machines bringing death to others and 'zero death' to one's own.

The mass crime was the exact inverse of the imperial brutality. It was sown to the latter like an inner lining, and its personnel, real or borrowed (Bin Laden, the Taliban, etc.), came directly from the cookhouses of the American hegemony; it had been educated and financed by the latter, its only desire was to have a preferable place in the latter's system. In such a configuration religion is nothing but a demagogic vocabulary worth neither more nor less than the fascist's populist 'anti-capitalism' slogans in the Thirties. One speaks for the 'disinherited' Muslims, but wants to become a billionaire Saudi Arabian, that is, an American, just as one claimed to be the mouthpiece of the 'German Worker' solely in order to become the devoted table companion of arms merchants. With Bush, one has God at one's side, along with the Good, Democracy, and also America (it's the same thing) for tracking down Evil – but in reality it is a matter of reminding all those disobedient imperial creatures that they will be reduced to ashes if they even think about undermining the Master. If not them, then their parents. Damn it, it's the aerial vendetta! And if not their parents, then the accursed villains with whom they live. And if not them then their hosts, no matter, any unfortunates vaguely resembling them will do! As the Defence Secretary, Rumsfeld, declared, with the frank speech of an imperialist on the hunt, it is a matter of killing as many people as possible. It must be said that some of those suave American professors lent him a helping hand in asking whether or not, considering the circumstances, it wouldn't be useful to use torture – to which some even more refined American professors objected that it would be in all respects preferable to expedite the suspects to allied countries in which torture was an official method. Upon the latest news, we hear that they are being rounded up, drugged and chained for transportation to the thousands of cells hastily constructed in a base at Guantanamo: on the island of Cuba, let's appreciate the irony.

In the same way as the crime of New York, America's war is unconnected to any law or right and is indifferent to any project. On both sides, it is a matter of striking blindly to demonstrate one's strike capacity. What is at stake are bloody and nihilistic games of power without purpose and without truth.

All the formal traits of the crime of New York indicate its nihilistic character: the sacralization of death; the absolute indifference to the victims; the transformation of oneself and others into instruments . . . but nothing speaks louder than the silence, the terrible silence of the authors and planners of this crime. For with affirmative, liberating, non-nihilistic political violence not only is responsibility always claimed, but its essence is found in claiming responsibility. In 1941, when the first resistance fighters killed a German officer or blew up a pylon, it was solely in order to be able to say 'it's us, the Resistance! Resistance exists and will continue to strike back!' The *tract*, saying who did what, however perilous it might be, must accompany the act. Violence is a *Trhact*. There is none of that today. The act remains unnamed and anonymous just like the culprits. There lies the infallible sign of a type of fascist nihilism.

Opposite it we find another nihilism for which an old name is appropriate, 'Capital'. *Das Kapital*: nihilist in its extensive form, the market having become worldwide; nihilist in its fetishization of the formalism of communication; and nihilist in its extreme political poverty, that is to say, in the absence of any project other than its perpetuation – the perpetuation of hegemony for the Americans and of vassalage, made as comfortable as possible, for the others.

At the level of structure, this nihilism could be called the nihilism of virtual equality. In one respect, the governments which are its servants organize monstrous inequalities, even in relation to life itself. If you are born in Africa you will probably live for around 30 years, whereas the figure is 80 if you are born in France. Such is the 'democratic' contemporary world. But at the same time (and this is what keeps the democratic fiction itself alive in the people's hearts and minds) there is an egalitarian dogmatism, that of an equality in their placement in front of commodities. The same product is offered everywhere. Armed with this universal commercial offer, contemporary 'democracy' can forge a subject from such abstract equality: the consumer; the one who, in his or her virtuality opposite the commodity, is ostensibly identical to any other in his or her abstract humanity as buying power. Man as shopping. As man (or woman) the consumer is the same as everyone else insofar as he or she looks at the same window display (that he or she has less money than others, and thus unequal buying power, is a secondary and contingent matter, and anyhow, it's no one's fault – save perhaps their own, if we look closely). The principle is that anyone who is able to buy – as a matter of right – anything being sold is the equal of anyone else.

However, as we all know, this equality is nothing but frustration and resentment. It is clearly the only equality that 'Western' governments and billionaire 'terrorists' can conjointly lay claim to.

At the level of circumstance, capitalist nihilism has arrived at a stage of the non-existence of any world. Yes, today there is no world, there is nothing but a group of singular disconnected situations. There is no world simply because the majority of the planet's inhabitants today do not even receive the gift of a name, of a simple name. When there was class society, proletarian parties (or those presumed to be such), the USSR, the national wars of liberation, etc., no matter which peasant in no matter what region – just as no matter which worker in no matter what town – could receive a political name. That is not to say that their material situation was better, certainly not, nor that that world was excellent. But symbolic positions existed, and that world was a world. Today, outside of the grand and petty bourgeoisie of the imperial cities, who proclaim themselves to be 'civilization', you have nothing apart from the anonymous and excluded. 'Excluded' is the sole name for those who have no name, just as 'market' is the name of a world which is not a world. In terms of the real, outside of the unremitting undertakings of those who keep thought alive, including political thinking, within a few singular situations, you have nothing apart from the American army.

H   To conclude: philosophy?

If the situation is as we say it is – the disjunctive synthesis of two nihilisms – then, as can be seen, it is formidable. It announces the repetition of disaster.

From this moment on, the task of philosophy is to welcome everything into thought which maintains itself outside that synthesis. Everything which affirmatively seizes a point of the real and raises it to the symbol will be taken by philosophy as a condition of its own becoming.

But to do that philosophy must break with whatever leads *it* into the circuits of nihilism, with everything that restrains and obliterates the power of the affirmative. It must go beyond the nihilistic motif of the 'end of Western metaphysics'. More generally, it must detach itself from the Kantian heritage, from the perpetual examination of limits, the critical obsession, and the narrow form of judgement. For one single thought has an immensity far beyond any judgement.

In a word: it is essential to break with the omnipresent motif of finitude. Its origins both critical and hermeneutical, as well regarded by the phenomenologists as by the positivists, the motif of finitude is the discrete form via which thought yields in advance, accepting the modest role it is enjoined to play, in all circumstances, by contemporary nihilism in all its ferocity.

The duty of philosophy is thus clear: to rationally reconstitute the reserve of the affirmative infinity that every liberating project requires. Philosophy does not have, and has never had at its own disposal the effective figures of emancipation. That is the primordial task of what is concentrated in political doing-thinking. Instead philosophy is like the attic where, in difficult times, one accumulates resources, lines up tools, and sharpens knives. Philosophy is exactly that which proposes an ample stock of means to other forms of thought. This time, it is on the side of affirmation and infinity that philosophy must select and accumulate its resources, its tools and its knives.

Notes

1   Translator's note: The first version of this paper was given at the Ecole Normale Supèrieure on 26 October 2001. We would like to acknowledge Steven Corcoran's translation, published in the journal *Theory and Event*, which was used as a base for the current translation. The original title was 'Philosophical considerations of some recent facts'.

2 Translator's note: In English the French *Occidentale* is translated by *Western*, but although the latter clearly designates the developed world, it does not resound as strongly with the second religious (Christian and Jewish) sense of the former. Thus, in anglophone countries it makes little sense to call a political group 'The Western Party', while in France during the 1960s and '70s, as Badiou recalls, 'l'Occident' was the name of an extreme right-wing party ...

3 Translator's note: 'Bougnoul' is a racist term which is employed in France to designate North-Africans or Arabs.

9
The definition of philosophy

Philosophy is prescribed by several conditions that are the types of truth procedures, or generic procedures.[1] These types are science (more precisely, the matheme), art (more precisely, the poem), politics (more precisely, politics in interiority or the politics of emancipation) and love (more precisely, the procedure that makes truth out of the disjunction of sexuated positions).

Philosophy is the place of thought where both the 'there are' [il y a] of truths and their compossibility is stated. In order to do this, philosophy sets up an operating category, Truth, which opens up an active void within thought. This void is located according to the inverse of a succession (the style of argumentative exposition) and the beyond of a limit (the style of persuasive, or subjectivizing, exposition). Philosophy, as discourse, thus organizes the superposition of a fiction of knowing and a fiction of art.

In the void opened by the gap or interval of these two fictionings, philosophy *seizes* truths. This seizure is its act. By this act, philosophy declares that there are truths, and ensures that thought is seized by this 'there are'. The seizure by the act attests to the unity of thought.

Fiction of knowing, philosophy imitates the matheme. Fiction of art, it imitates the poem. Intensity of an act, it is like a love without object. Addressed to all such that all may *be* within the seizure of the existence of truths, it is like a political strategy without the stakes of power.

Via this quadruple discursive imitation, philosophy knots the system of its conditions into itself. This is the reason why *a* philosophy is homogenous to its epoch's stylistics. Nonetheless, this permanent contemporaneity orients itself not towards empirical time, but towards what Plato calls 'the always of time', towards the intemporal essence of time that philosophy names eternity. The philosophical seizure of truths exposes them to eternity; one could say, with Nietzsche, to the eternity of their *return*. This eternal exposition is all the more real in that the truths are seized in the extreme urgency and extreme precariousness of their temporal trajectory.

The act of seizure, such as an eternity orientates it, tears truths from the straightjacket of sense; it *separates* them from the law of the world. Philosophy is subtractive, in that it makes a hole in sense, or interrupts – such that the truths may all be *said* together – the circulation of sense. Philosophy is a senseless act; yet, in that, it is rational.

Philosophy is never an interpretation of experience. It is the act of Truth in regard to truths. And this act, which, according to the law of the world, is unproductive (it does not produce even one truth), places a subject without object, open solely to the truths that pass in its seizing.

Let us call 'religion' everything which supposes a continuity between truths and the circulation of sense. Philosophy, then, against all hermeneutics, that is, against the religious law of sense, sets out compossible truths on the basis of the void. It thus subtracts thought from every presupposition of a Presence.

The subtractive operations by which philosophy seizes these truths 'outside sense' come under four modalities: the undecidable, which relates to the event (a truth is not, it occurs); the indiscernible, which relates to freedom (the trajectory of a truth is not constrained, but hazardous); the generic, which relates to being (the being of a truth is an infinite set subtracted from every predicate of knowledge); and the unnameable, which relates to the Good (forcing the nomination of an unnameable engenders disaster).

The schema of connection of the four subtractive figures (undecidable, indiscernible, generic and unnameable) specifies a philosophical doctrine of the Truth. This schema lays out the thought of the void on the basis of which truths are seized.

Every philosophical process is polarized by a specific adversary, the sophist. The sophist is externally (or discursively) indiscernible from the philosopher, since his operation also combines fictions of knowledge and fictions of art. Subjectively, the two are opposed, because the sophist's linguistic strategy aims at doing without any positive assertion concerning truths. In this sense, we can also define philosophy as the act by which indiscernible discourses are nevertheless opposed, or rather as what separates itself from its double. Philosophy is always the breaking of a mirror. This mirror is the surface of language, upon which the sophist places everything which philosophy deals with in its act. If the philosopher would contemplate himself upon this surface alone, then he will see his double, the sophist, emerge there, and thereby he could take the latter for himself.

This relation to the sophist exposes philosophy internally to a temptation whose effect is to divide it again. Because the desire to finish with the sophist *once and for all* impedes the seizure of truths: 'once and for all' inevitably means that Truth annuls the chance of truths, and that philosophy wrongfully declares itself productive of truths. Through such a declaration *being*-true ends up in the position of stand-in for the *act* of Truth.

A triple effect of the sacred, of ecstasy and terror thereby corrupts the philosophical operation, and can lead it from the aporetic void that sustains its act to criminal prescriptions. By which philosophy induces every disaster in thought.

The ethics of philosophy, which wards off disaster, consists entirely in a constant *reserve* with regard to its sophistic double, a reserve which allows philosophy to remove itself from the temptation of dividing itself (according to the couple void/substance) in order to deal with its original foundational duplicity (sophist/philosopher).

The history of philosophy is the history of its ethics: a succession of violent gestures via which philosophy has withdrawn itself from its disastrous reduplication. Or rather: philosophy in its history is nothing more than a desubstantialization of the Truth, which is also the auto-liberation of its act.

Note

1   This paper appears in the collection, A. Badiou, *Conditions* (Paris: Seuil, 1992), 79–82.

10
Ontology and politics

An interview with Alain Badiou

OF: Can you elaborate your concept of structure, given that you identify it as the operator of the count-for-one of a situation?[1]

AB: The problem is how a multiplicity becomes consistent. There are two responses to this question: first, at the level of presentation and, second, at the level of representation. Structure is the name I give to the combination of the two levels, presentation *and* representation. Structure is not the same thing as the state of a situation because the state of the situation is only the second level, the level of representation. Structure includes the first level of presentation, belonging, and the second level also – the state, the second count-for-one. Structure, I think, has two determinations and not one determination. The first is the level of presentation, which only designates that some sort of multiplicity is in the situation. The second level, the state, of inclusion, designates that multiplicity is not corrupted by the void. Structure consists of both levels.

OF: Can one ask what counts-for-one a situation? Does it make sense to ask what *performs* the operation of the count-for-one of the situation? Is there an agent?

AB: The operation is the situation itself. The operation is not distinct from the multiplicity in itself. There is no presentation of multiplicity *and* the operation. The operation *is* the same thing as the presentation. It is possible that this terminology is not very good and I have to change it, because the real problem is the variation between being and being-there. It's a problem of the localization of being and not only a problem of structure or of the count-for-one. In the work in progress, the terminology is reworked, though the count-for-one remains a part of my thinking.[2] But the true problem is the question of the localization of being, and, which requires the introduction of other concepts than presentation, representation and so on.

OF: It appears to be the privilege of the situation of ontology that the registers of unity and identity are clearly separated. Are they necessarily fused in your account of the structures of non-ontological situations?

AB: I don't think there is at this point a privilege of the situation [of ontology] because in every situation in thinking the problem of unity and of identity are indiscernible. I have to elaborate the question of identity from the question of the unity of the multiplicity – it's the same thing. The unity of the multiplicity *is* the ontological identity. And this point is true in the ontological situation, mathematics, because one set is the identity of a multiplicity, but it's the same thing in other situations because I don't concern myself with qualitative identity.

OF: How can non-ontological situations be differentiated if not on the basis of some universal language into which they are all translated?

AB: The difference between situations is a matter of experience. We have to distinguish situations from the point of view of truth – an anonymous situation – and situations from the point of view of knowledge. From the point of view of knowledge, the situations are different on the basis of experiences and the encyclopaedia of knowledge. I name this sort of difference 'predicative difference', and there are predicative differences between situations. This is not very different to the fact that, I don't know, a horse is not a cat. In a situation there is always a distribution of predicates which establish this sort of difference. From the point of view of truth, situations are seized in their being and the difference becomes ontological difference. Here we have to think that the multiplicity of the situation is not the same as another multiplicity. The set is not the same. The type of infinity is not the same but all these considerations are only practicable from the point of view of the process of the truth, and not from the point of view of the encyclopaedia of knowledge.

JC: It's clear that these points of view are very different – the point of view of knowledge which is obviously in a situation, names, predicates, cats, horses, etc., and the point of view of truth, which is not predicative, indiscernible in a situation, etc. A truth, for you, is universal. And since truth is rare, it doesn't always happen: not every situation is truthful. Is then the inverse possible, that in a situation everyone has access to knowledge?

AB: In a situation the access to knowledge is different for different people, for different beings. But my thesis is that in a situation there is always an encyclopaedia of knowledge which is the same for everybody. But the access to this knowledge is very different. We can speak in Marxist terms, we can say that in a situation there is an ideological *dispositif* [apparatus] which is dominant – in the end it's the same thing.

JC: Would you say Marxism talks about encyclopaedic knowledges but doesn't talk about the truth?

AB: No, no I think that in Marxism, the category of Marxism designates the same thing that I designate by the *dispositif* of the encyclopaedia of knowledge. But in Marxism also there is a series of truths, which is different from ideology.

GB: Can I ask a related question? This is a very naive question. How can you avoid decisionism? And, if I could explain that, I remember in George Lukacs, *History and Class Consciousness*, he says, 'Decisions, real decisions, precede the facts,' but from the point of view of Marxism he can understand the entirety of bourgeois knowledge and supersede it. As you recall the standing point of totality is one that is both ontological and takes in the entirety of bourgeois knowledge. So, after the decision is made, there *is* a basis for knowing that you have taken the right decision and a basis for discussion with other people who are not yet Marxists. Would you agree with Lukacs? Once the decision is made is there a basis for knowing that you have made the right decision?

AB: I think there is no decisionism at all in my philosophy. There is a complete misreading on this point. Lyotard said that I was an absolute decisionist, a sort of new Carl Schmitt. But I think there's some confusion here because, after all, the crucial question is the event and the event is not the result of a decision. The difficulty is that in *L'Etre et l'événement*, I say that the name of the event is the matter of a pure decision and I have to change that point. It's not very good terminology, the terminology of the nomination. I now think that the event has consequences, objective consequences and logical consequences. These consequences are separated by the event. The effect of the event is a profound transformation of the logic of the situation – and that is not an effect of decision. The decision is uniquely to be faithful to the transformation. So, you can have a discussion with other people about the logical consequences of being or not being faithful [to the event]. What the consequences are in and about the situation involves a rational discussion, and this is not so different from the Marxist conception in which you can say that practice is a mix of decision and theoretical control of decisions. In the current form of my work I don't attribute the decision to the name of the event, but to the event directly and, finally, to the logical consequences of the event. This is part of a transformation of my concept of the subject. It is not exactly the same as in *L'Etre et l'événement*. So, I am not a decisionist at all ... now.

OF: There are some questions related to this discussion. In *L'Etre et l'événement*, you say: 'In the same situation, and for the same event, different criteria [of connection] could exist which define different fidelities.'[3] How would a local contest between two generic procedures be anything other than a contest of power and interpretations? From a perspective immanent to a historical situation, what would mark a generic procedure as genuinely generic? You have said a non-generic authoritarian or theological position would fuse truth and sense – could you explain by example?

AB: It is necessary to recognize that nothing attests that a generic procedure is authentically generic. On this point I have the same conception of truth as Spinoza. Truth is an *index sui*. Truth is the proof of itself. There is no external guarantee. So, the genericity of the procedure of truth is effective in the process itself. This point is very important because major philosophical differences are linked to it. For very different thinkers – Heidegger, Lacan, Spinoza, Deleuze, myself – there is a conviction that truth has no guarantee, and for other analytical philosophers it is necessary for truth to have guarantees in thought and judgement. It is the principal split today.

OF: So, say I'm faithful to an event and engaged in a generic procedure and there are some other people who think they are in the same historical situation and who are faithful to the event in another generic procedure. How would we judge each other or is there just conflict?

AB: There is no abstract answer to that sort of problem. It is a matter of the concrete situation. If I am faithful to a political event, after May '68 on the one hand, and on the other hand I am in love with a woman, well, that's my situation. There is no abstract possibility for grasping this sort of situation. There is no problem at all in fact. The situation is always traversed by different generic procedures at different levels which concern different situations, an infinity of multiplicities and so on. That is the concrete analysis of the situation. It is not an ontological problem.

OF: If *a* generic procedure is the truth of a situation do generic procedures traverse more than one situation?

AB: Two generic procedures are never actually in the same situation of reference because they are truths of their situations. But a concrete situation is not exactly the ontological scheme of the situation. A concrete situation is an interplay of different situations in the ontological sense of the term. Ontology is not by itself the thinking of a concrete situation. Ontology is *a* situation, the ontological situation which is the situation of thinking, and finally, the mathematical situation. We can think a part of the concrete situation from the ontological schema. We can say, there is a multiplicity, it is infinite and so on. But there is a concrete analysis which is not ontological at all. Ontology is not Hegel's absolute knowledge!

JC: If that's the case then there are no subjects, in your sense, working within a situation. To explain that, is there a super-Christian subject within the religious situation? For example, it's not an individual person who is a subject in your sense, because they enter into the process of *becoming* a subject. Is there one 'über-subject' or 'ultra-subject' that we can consider 'Christian' that's still faithful to the event of Christ? A subject which has lasted over 2000 years and which *is* that subject in its very slow vanishing (in our terms) – but in your terms? Can you consider the subject in these terms?

AB: I don't think so. There is no super subject. A subject is a subject of a definite situation, the Occidental situation from the Roman Empire and so on. There is a particularity of the situation and the subject is a particular subject. The philosophical category of the subject has very different referents. In the situation of political organization there can be a subject, in another situation there is a subject of love which is different, in a third situation the Christian subject, it's another thing, and so on. So, there is great complexity in the category of subject and the semantics of this category is very diverse.

OF: A related question. In *Théorie du sujet* you embrace Heiner Muller's maxim: 'For something to come, something must go', and say that destruction is a necessary partner of creation. Yet in *L'Etre et l'événement*, you change your position and say that any violence arises from the state of the situation and is not a necessary part of the generic procedure. Why the change?

AB: I think that in *Théorie du sujet* destruction is a dialectical concept. Destruction signifies that a part of the situation can be destroyed for the new, for the event. It is sometimes necessary. I don't say in *L'Etre et l'événement* that destruction is always a bad thing. It can be necessary to destroy something for the newness of the event. But I don't think it is a necessary part of the newness. Because I think the newness is a supplementation and not a destruction. It is something which happens, something which comes, and this point is the crucial point. It is possible that for the becoming of the newness something has to be destroyed but it is not the essence, the being, the kernel of the process. It can just be a consequence. In *Théorie du sujet* I thought that negativity was creative in itself and I don't think that now. I think that creativity is a sort of affirmation and not a sort of negation.

JC: Can you then think if, say, destruction and the event are independent of each other, destruction may or may not be part of that event, but in a sense destruction may be an essential part of *an* event? Sometimes destruction will be part of an event; can you be faithful to the consequences of that destruction? For example, in the French Revolution, following all the consequences of the Terror may have been legitimate and ethical.

AB: It is always possible that destruction takes place amongst the consequences of an event. You can't always avoid destruction. It's a part of the particularity of an event, the relation between destruction and affirmation. In political events this relation is very difficult to think and control. In political events and generic processes the violence is always there because many people don't like newness. The transformation of the situation is always against some people – rich men, men in power. In political truth the relation between, on the one hand, destruction and violence, and on the other hand, affirmation and supplementation, is a complex relation. I think that in *Théorie du sujet*, political truth was paradigmatic for me. When I wrote 'destruction is necessary', it was because political truth was the point. But if we take another paradigm it appears that destruction is a particularity of the consequences of the political event but not an internal characteristic of the process of truth in itself.

OF: In *L'Etre et l'événement* you say: 'The heterogeneity of language games is at the base of the diversity of situations. Being is unfolded in multiple ways because its unfolding is only presented in the multiple of languages' (321-2). What must be added to this to distinguish it from what you precisely characterize as the ontology of 'idealinguistery' (linguistic idealism)?

AB: Yes, yes, it is a sort of citation of Wittgenstein, a sort of strange beast between Wittgenstein and me. The text is not very good. The idea is simple. The idea is that being in a situation, you have predicative diversity in the encyclopaedia of knowledge and the difference between parts of a situation is always seized by predicative difference; the language of the situation is the medium of knowledge. From the point of view of knowledge, it is the source of difference. But finally the true differences are the differences of the sets themselves, of the multiplicities. So the text is only saying that in the knowledge of the situation we have an access to differences by the medium of language, by the medium of predicates. So difference in knowledge is predicative. Naturally, it is not my thinking that language constitutes differences. There is an access via language to difference in knowledge – first point – but language doesn't constitute the ontological differences, not at all. And when we have the capacity of having the point of view of truth we understand that the differences which are ontological differences are absolutely distinct from predicative differences. 'Idealinguistery', linguistic idealism, on the other hand, consists in thinking that language constitutes differences. From my point of view this is to fuse knowledge and truth. We always have to separate truth from knowledge or, in Marx's language, truth from ideology, or in Plato's language, truth from *doxa*, to have an access to the real and when we don't separate truth from knowledge we don't have access to the real and then we have the possibility of declaring that language constitutes differences. But the key point is the difference between knowledge and truth, and I have to insist that this is the crucial point of philosophical discussion today. I am more and more convinced of this.

OF: To return to ontological schemas. What says that a particular situation has a certain ontological schema? What criteria can be used to judge this given that all non-ontological qualities of the situation have been subtracted when it is written in ontology? That is, we know how to proceed from non-ontological situations to the situation of ontology – abstraction, subtraction – but how can the ontological difference be traversed in the other direction (in a positive manner)?

AB: It's the same problem! There is just one question, and it is, 'What is the difference between different situations?' I think it is *the* question – for you! The moment of thinking from concrete situations is by subtraction and abstraction and the question is how are we going [can we go] in the other direction, from ontology to concrete situations. But I think we don't have to go in the other direction. We have a concrete situation. We can think the ontological structure of that situation. We can! It is very difficult sometimes, but we can. So we can think about infinite multiplicity, something about the natural multiplicity, something about the historical character of the situation, something about the evental site and so on. There is an ontological schema of the situation. With this schema we can understand the situation. The crucial point is, are we able to understand the situation from the point of view of truth or only from the point of view of knowledge? If we can understand the situation from the point of view of truth then there is a process of truth which is irreducible to the ontological categories. Because when the subject is constituted in the concrete development of a truth, he or she experiences the situation, directly, and that sort of experience has nothing to do with ontology. When we are in a political fight, or in love, or in a concrete artistic creation we are not in the ontological situation.

DR: Are you saying then that it is impossible to understand a situation ontologically without prior experience or knowledge of the ontological essence of a situation?

AB: My conviction is that everybody who is engaged in faithfulness in the relation to an event has an understanding of the situation. So it is not a prerequisite to have prior knowledge. Prior knowledge is always necessary to understand the being, the ontological schema of the situation, the mathematical categories and so on, because we have to work for that sort of understanding; terrible work! But from the point of view of singular truth we have an access from the event itself and not from preconstituted knowledge. The truth creates the understanding of the process of truth and the subject *is* this sort of understanding. So, the truth needs nothing other than itself. It's very important. The truth is not a question of knowledge; it is the *defection* of knowledge. This is the reason why the people who defend knowledge are against events: the subject which is constituted within a truth, in a way, has no need of knowledge. Such a subject *is* a transformation of knowledge, a complete transformation of knowledge.

GB: What happens when the real event lies in the future – Lenin in 1917? Could you explain your understanding of Lenin in 1917? Because you can say that Lenin was faithful before the Russian Revolution, to 1905.

AB: Lenin explained that he was faithful to the Commune of Paris. There is always an event for faithfulness and we know that when the Russian Revolution lasted longer than the Paris Commune, Lenin danced on the snow! The constitution of Lenin as a subjective revolutionary depends on the fact that, in contrast to Trotsky and others, he was not faithful to Marxism – he was a Marxist, naturally – but he was not faithful to Marxism, he was faithful to the French Revolution and the Paris Commune – it's another thing. It's a very important point and it is the same question. Knowledge is important, but the faithfulness which constitutes the subject – the revolutionary subject, the political subject – is not made of knowledge but made of other things than knowledge. In the case of Lenin it is very interesting. On the one hand, Lenin was in the middle of the people who were Marxists in the first years of the twentieth century yet, on the other hand, he refers systematically to events and not exclusively to the doctrine or theory.

AL: You seem to situate the question of the event as a historical phenomenon and I was reminded when you were speaking of Lacan's comment in *Encore* where he compares Lenin's relation to Marx with his own in relation to Freud. It's interesting to think about the relation of fidelity and truth not so much in relation to a political or cultural event but to an event in thought itself. Is that something you would consider?

AB: Yes. The case of Lacan is very clear. Lacan says that the American psychoanalysis was not faithful to Freud and that his faithfulness is a faithfulness to Freud, not Freud as a person, not even as a theory, but as an event in thinking, of universal thinking. Lacan thought that the majority of psychoanalysts had forgotten that event. So there are events in thinking, I agree with you. There is an example which is very clear for me. Just before the Renaissance Greek mathematics were forgotten, especially the writings of Archimedes. It is very surprising to see that Greek mathematics in the Renaissance and in the first years of the 1700s were constituted as a faithfulness to Archimedes – after a long obscurity since the text had existed but nobody could read it. The Renaissance was the capacity to be faithful in reading to these absolutely forgotten and obscure writings.

OF: In *L'Etre et l'événement* you argue that historicity is constituted by events and generic procedures. You also talk of the modern epochal decision as to the infinity of being. How exactly would you distance yourself from Heidegger's history of being?

AB: If history is constituted by events and generic truths there is no unified history, there is nothing like 'History'. There are historical sequences, a multiplicity of historical sequences. If I say, for example, that there is a sequence after Galileo, of modern physics, then I think the event of the creation of modern mathematical physics opens a sequence of the thinking or understanding of Nature. That sort of thing has nothing to do with the Heideggerean conviction of a monumental history of being from the Greeks until the present day with its sequences of the forgetting of being, metaphysics, nihilism and so on. I think it is necessary to speak of historicity and not of a History. I think there is a profound historicity of truth, which is quite natural, since truth is a process and not a donation. But there is not *a* History of being or *a* History of truth; rather there are histories of truths, of the multiplicity of truths. So, I am neither Hegelian, nor Heideggerean! Because the common feature of Hegel and Heidegger's thought is precisely that of thinking there is *a* History of being and thought.

OF: Why do you say all or almost all situations are infinite when set theory does not say that all sets are infinite? How do you move from saying the modern decision that being is infinite to: (1) there is an infinity of situations, and then to (2) every situation is infinite?

AB: When I say that all situations are infinite, it's an axiom. It is impossible to deduce this point. It is an axiomatic conviction, a modern conviction. I think it is better to think that all situations are infinite. It is better for thinking to say that situations are infinite. Because we come after a long philosophical period in which the theme of finitude and the conviction that all situations are finite was dominant, and we are suffering the effects of that sort of conviction. For example, for a long time, Marxism itself had the conviction that all situations could be reduced to finite parameters: two-class struggle, dominant ideology, imperialism versus socialism and so on. Today, with a great deal of caution, we must draw as a conclusion a sort of ethics of thinking from that history. The ethics of thinking today is to say that it is better to think that all situations are infinite, that it is very difficult to reduce a situation to finite parameters. It is a conviction. It is not a deduction. Naturally, from the point of view of the strictest ontology, there is no necessity to say that all situations are infinite, because finite multiplicities exist. But the question is not there, the question is not purely objective. In pure objectivity it is always possible to say there are finite situations. In fact, a lot of philosophers say precisely that, that situations are finite. Such is the theme of the essential finitude of the human being. I think it is necessary to work against that kind of conviction. The consequences of the fact that situations are infinite – we don't know them very well. It is a new axiom. It constitutes a rupture to say that situations are infinite and that human life is infinite and that we are infinite. It is a new axiom and we have to explore its consequences. It is more interesting and more attuned to the necessity of the times than declaring that we are finite and all is finite, we are mortal beings, being for death and so on. We are being-for-the-infinite.

LM: So your mathematics supports that, that's what you're saying?

AB: Yes. Absolutely. If my ontology is linked with mathematics, as you know, the theme of infinity is most important in that link. Because mathematics is the only rational thinking of infinity. The story of infinity has been marked by theological thinking for a long, long time. We must liberate this category from the theological conception, and mathematics is the unique means for doing so. We must think the infinity of the situations without the theological conception. It is possible only today, now, for us, with mathematics and this is why I often say one philosophical task is to be faithful to Cantor. This faithfulness to Cantor is not yet accomplished.

OF: One classic question for a philosopher. Doesn't any ontology have to include an account of its applicability to non-ontological situations? For example, doesn't any ontology have to attempt to explain why science works?

AL: It is related to why you think mathematics is the answer to this question of infinity.

AB: There are two different questions. The first question is: Is ontology able or not to explain science and the functions of science? The second question is: Why is mathematics necessary in ontology itself? It is not the same question.

OF: No. Just one question, because for Andrew mathematics is a science itself. Doesn't any ontology have to attempt to explain why science functions, for example, why we can send man to the moon and back?

AB: Yes. The difficulty in my conception is that ontology has to explain why science operates but ontology is mathematics, so mathematics has to explain how mathematics operates and it is a real problem, a real problem. A large part of *L'Etre et l'événement* tries to explain with the means of mathematics why mathematics is ontology. As a matter of fact it is its task. We must say for example, if being is inconsistent multiplicity the consequence of this thesis is that ontology is necessarily a sort of set theory, a consistent theory of inconsistent multiplicity. We have a complex relation between ontology and science, in my case ontology and mathematics, in the case of Kant between ontology and physics. There is a complex relation between ontology and science because there is an ontological status of science itself. So philosophical categories are appropriate for thinking the relation between science as science and science as an ontological enterprise. This question has been a part of philosophy since the Greeks; it is not particular to my philosophy. One part of philosophy is to organize discussion between science and science. In Plato we can say that there is a discussion between Greek mathematics and Greek mathematics, a philosophical discussion between the mathematics of the working mathematicians and mathematics as part of thinking being itself. In *L'Etre et l'événement* the same thing occurs. There is a philosophical discussion between set theory as a mathematical creation and set theory as an ontological thinking. Science doesn't organize that discussion. This is the reason why philosophy is necessary. Science doesn't include an evaluation of its double nature. Philosophy is able to organize the discussion between science and science or to think the double nature of science, mathematics or physics, or biology (which is the case for Aristotle). A large part of Aristotle's work is devoted to a discussion between biology and the science of the being of living beings.

This is also the case with Bergson, who mounts a philosophical discussion between the theory of life and the theory of life. It is a very important point. There is no intrinsic relation between science and philosophy. Philosophy is not an interpretation of science. Philosophy is the method for organizing the discussion between science and science, science on the side of specific production and science as a part of the thinking of being *qua* being.

OF: A question on modality. In your article on Wittgenstein there is a passage on the relation between being and the laws of existence, the 'mondanité du monde' [the worldhood of the world]. What is it that regulates the fact that there are certain situations which exist? The question is: What will be the role of modality in your new work? Are you developing another logic of modality or another modal ontology?

AB: It is a terrible question. The question is more complex than anything I have ever written! No, but I understand it very well. In my philosophy there are two instances of contingency and so of modality. First in a situation there is no reason for the existence of that situation. I am not Leibnizean. I don't think there is a principle of sufficient reason. There is an irreducible contingency to a situation because, on the one hand, there is no intrinsic interior mark of the necessity of the situation. On the other hand, the event itself is marked by contingency. There is a double contingency of truth: the contingency of the situation of which it is the truth, and the contingency of the event of which the truth is the process of consequences. The ontology of truth, the thinking of the being of the truth, is a theory of modality. In the work in progress, the second book of *L'Etre et l'événement*, which I am going to publish one day, I have to explain that the process of truth is not necessary but contingent. The consequences of such contingency for the concept of truth will then have to be explained because in the philosophical tradition truth is always linked to necessity and not to contingency. This question is a logical question because truth, in my conviction, is a transformation – not of the being of a situation, because its being remains the same – but of the logic of the situation. A truth is a transformation of the articulation of the multiplicity of the situation – its logic – and this transformation is linked to contingency, both of the event and of the situation. A truth doesn't express a necessity of the situation. It expresses the contingency of the situation, the sort of contingency which is linked to the central ontological void of the situation. All of a situation's characteristics are affected by the transformation of its logic. It is thus necessary to explain what a logical transformation is when you move from one logic to another logic. This movement from a logic to another logic is the real effect of truth procedures. It is only possible to understand this movement if we have a solid conception of the logic of a situation. The logic of a situation is different to its being. We have to think not only multiplicity but also multiplicity here – not *sein*, but *da-sein*. The logic is of the *da*, of here, of localization. Localization requires a sort of transcendental conception of the situation. I can demonstrate that the logic of the situation is a sort of modal logic. It's between classical logic – because being in itself is classical, set theory is classical – but the logic of the situation, of the localized multiplicity, that sort of logic is between classical logic and intuitionist logic. This is a technical question, but not so technical that it is impossible to explain!

JC: If that's the case and you have to think that truth in the classical sense is always necessary, then in classical philosophy there's no dispute possible about the force of the truth – the truth is maybe *pure* force. It's necessary, it's unavoidable. However, if truth is contingent, then you are left with the question of the force of a truth in a situation and the differences between a big event and a little event, in terms of force. Is there then a possible meta-logical, or meta-ontological way to talk about the contingency of the *force* of an event?

AB: The distinction between events is always a distinction between the consequences of events because an event in itself is always a perfect weakness. It is such because the being of an event is to disappear; the being of an event is disappearing. The event is nothing – just a sort of illumination – but the consequences of an event within a situation are always very different and it is true that there are major consequences, long sequences of truth, or brief sequences. There are a large variety of truths. The means for interpreting this sort of difference is the transformation of the logical apparatus of the situation. It is possible in my elaboration of this question, to evaluate the difference between a large transformation and a weak logical transformation. It is perfectly possible.

JC: Is it also a qualitative difference? Are there different beings of the truth of different events? Can, then, if you are talking about a transformation in the logic of situations, and each situation has a truth and there is a being of that truth, maybe you can talk about big or small events and these are quantitative differences? Are there qualitative differences in the being of truths of different situations?

AB: It is possible to treat that sort of difference as qualitative difference because they concern the appearance of the situation. The second book of *L'Etre et l'événement* – which doesn't exist at all! – treats appearance, which is the name for the logical constitution of the situation. In this book I transform the concept of situation which in *L'Etre et l'événement* is only thought from the point of view of pure multiplicity: this gives an ontological conception of situation. In the second book there is the same ontological conception of the situation but I have to explain that the situation is not only a multiplicity but also a multiplicity-here – *sein-da* – a localized multiplicity, and not localized from the point of view of totality because there is no such totality. There is a characteristic of multiplicity which is that of being *here*, and it is necessarily internal to the situation: such is the appearing of the situation or its logical constitution, it's the same thing. So when we say that the consequences of an event are significant, we are saying the logical transformation of the situation can be evaluated from the situation itself as an important transformation and the norm of that sort of evaluation is in that situation itself, not outside it. Important or unimportant can be said from inside the situation.

RH: This follows on from Justin's question and from the example of Lenin. If there's a fidelity or faithfulness to the event, surely unfaithfulness to the event can always be faithfulness to another event? Which is also a question related to the ontological difference.

AB: Unfaithfulness for me is always what happens to a faithfulness. Unfaithfulness is only something thinkable from the point of view of already having faithfulness ...

IV: There's no unfaithfulness as such, you always have to have first faithfulness and then you get unfaithfulness. You can't be unfaithful as such.

AB: If in a situation somebody doesn't care about the event at all it is not, in my words, unfaithfulness, it is indifference and indifference is always a form of reaction to the event. In my current elaboration I name this position the reactive subject. The reactive subject is the subject who says the event is not important and so on, but that is not unfaithfulness, it is a sort of indifference. Unfaithfulness is when a subject is constituted by faithfulness but that faithfulness disappears.

IV: He renounces his fidelity, a sort of treason.

AB: Yes, unfaithfulness is renunciation.

RH: Is that faithfulness to another event?

IV: No.

AB: I think it is not a faithfulness to another event.

RH: So renunciation is not an event?

IV: No. I am very sorry.

OF: Three more questions. First, Louis has a question about the Holocaust.

LM: You wrote at the beginning of the *Manifesto* that certain contemporary philosophers are perhaps conceited in their persistent response to the question of the Holocaust. My question is: How shall we view your response to that? Can we indeed suggest, or view your response, as perhaps a conceited response as well, in that you would wish – not necessarily incorrectly, but perhaps incorrectly – to move on or to attempt to move on, a 'new philosophy'? You wrote that around 1989. How would you view that now, the question of the conceitedness of those French philosophers?

AB: The difficulty of the problem is that the question of Auschwitz and the Holocaust is in my opinion a profound political question which has not yet been clarified. In my opinion the philosophical discourse about it is a substitute for the lack of a political treatment of the question. Many philosophers have said that after Auschwitz it is impossible to philosophize or that great philosophy has crashed and so on. But I think this is not the true problem. The true problem is that for complex reasons there has been no political treatment of the question of what happened in the Nazi period. When I say that it is necessary to take one step further, I want to say two different things. The first one is that it is not possible for philosophy to have, about the question of Auschwitz, the Holocaust and the Nazi period, a better discourse than other thinkings. It is a political question; we are obliged to assign this question to historical and political thinking. Philosophy is able to elaborate some categories about the

Holocaust, naturally, and in my *Ethics* I try to do something about that, but it is not the crucial point. The crucial point today is what is, after Auschwitz, after the crash of the socialist state and so on, what is a political task? Is there or is there not a politics of emancipation? Are we all buried in the capitalist period forever?! The second point is that I don't think it is acceptable to say that because of the history of the century philosophy is impossible or absolutely consummated. So when I say 'one step further' it is simply a manner of saying I don't believe in the discourse of the end, the end of philosophy and so on. Because I prefer affirmation to negation, I prefer to talk of trying to make a step rather than always saying philosophy is bad, or impossible, and as such paralysing philosophy.

OF: To finish we have two questions on love.

AL: This is a question that came from some passages in the *Manifesto* where you discuss Lacan and his contribution to the philosophical use of love. You say in those passages almost that Lacan was a theorist of love despite himself. It's interesting to consider that first of all, but second of all to consider what Lacan thought he was, a theoretician of desire and the unconscious. I wondered why you singled out, why you take love from Lacan rather than the Freudian subversion, the unconscious.

AB: I extract love from Lacan because I think love from Plato onwards is a specific condition of philosophy. I understand perfectly that Lacan is a theoretician of desire and of the unconscious, and the field of psycho-analysis. But there are also many texts and interventions about love in Lacan's work: and I think that the situation of the Lacanian text about love is complex, complete with formal contradictions; it is very interesting ... I was just saying that, as philosophers, we have to, if we want, assume the experience of love as a condition of philosophy. Plato says the same thing in the *Symposium*. To do this, we have to assume the Lacanian hypotheses concerning love, which are very complex and very new. Lacan's conception of love is not the same as that of Freud. Naturally it is the same thing with desire and the unconsciousness but with love, it's not at all the same thing. Lacan distinguishes love and desire in philosophical terms because he says that love is connected with being and desire is connected with the object, it's not exactly the same thing. This is why, I think, that all philosophers who assume that love is a condition of philosophy have to sustain the experience of the Lacanian text on love.

OF: Last question. Justin, it's yours about faithfulness, you know, isn't faithfulness itself an act of love ...?

AB: (*To Justin*) You don't know your own question?

JC: I can barely remember my own name ... It's more to do with the question of fidelity and its possible identity with love. For you it seems absolutely crucial that love, mathematics, politics, they're absolutely separate, absolutely heterogeneous, they don't intermingle with each other in any way, yet in 'What is love?' there are two sexuated positions, there's man who metaphorizes, and woman who knots the four truth-processes together. Insofar as these are a knotting – that is, in fidelity to an event of love a woman knots all of these – is one not in love when one is faithful to a political event?

AB: The problem is the problem of the connection between the different procedures. It is a problem which is very interesting and complex. For instance, there are some similarities between politics and love, and I demonstrate this with technical concepts, numericity and the unname-able and so on; a singular connection between artistic creation and political thought also, and also a connection between love and science because love and science are the two procedures which don't know that they are procedures, in fact. It is not the same with artistic creation. We know perfectly that it is a procedure of truth in rivalry with science. It is not the same, naturally, for the other conditions. It is necessary to elaborate a general theory of the connections of the knots between different procedures but the difficult point is to have criteria for such an evaluation: however, it is possible once you have categories for the different steps of the procedures. I am working on this point. There are some texts in *Conditions*. The crucial concepts are the concept of the numericity of the procedure and the concepts of the connection of the procedure with the event, the undecidable, the indiscernible, the unnameable, and the nature of the stopping point of the procedure. With all of these categories it is possible and necessary to have a thinking of the different connections between different procedures of truths. As you remark, there is some connection between politics and love, it's an old story because, for example, all the French tragedies, Racine, Corneille, speak about the link between love and politics, a perfect example. In Lacan, for example, we find some connection, very interesting, between love and science. The link between politics and artistic creation is very elaborate, for example, in the work of Deleuze. It's a very interesting field.

Notes

1 This interview took place on 8 September 1999, at the University of Melbourne. The discussion was in English. Participants in the interview included – aside from Badiou himself – Isabelle Vodoz, Geoff Boucher, Justin Clemens, Ralph Humphries, Oliver Feltham, Andrew Lewis, Louis Magee and Dan Ross. Insofar as the questioners could be identified from the tape-recording, their initials appear in the body of the text. Aside from minor grammatical emendations, the transcript of the interview has been reproduced here in its entirety.

2 Editor's note: Badiou was referring to the companion volume to *L'Etre et l'événement*, whose current title stands as *Logiques des mondes* (Logics of worlds), forthcoming from Editions du Seuil.

3 Alain Badiou, *L'Etre et l'événement* (Paris: Seuil, 1988), 258–9.

Index of Names